Toons that Teach

75 CARTOON MOMENTS TO GET TEENAGERS TALKING

STEVEN CASE

ZONDERVAN™

WWW.ZONDERVAN.COM

Youth Specialties

www.youthspecialties.com

Dedication:

One of the fondest memories of my childhood is of my brother and me sitting on my father's lap as we watched Road Runner cartoons. The Coyote would fall off the cliff and land on the ground in that little puff of smoke, and my father would laugh every time. My brother and I would giggle, because we'd feel his whole body shake beneath us.

This book is for my father.

Youth Specialties

Toons That Teach: 75 Cartoon Moments to Get Kids Talking
Copyright © 2005 by Youth Specialties

Youth Specialties Products, 300 South Pierce Street, El Cajon, CA 92020, are published
by Zondervan, 5300 Patterson Avenue SE, Grand Rapids, MI 49530

Library of Congress Cataloging-in-Publication Data

Case, Steven, 1964-
  Toons that teach : 75 cartoon moments to get kids talking / by Steven Case.
    p. cm.
  Includes indexes.
  ISBN 0-310-25992-4 (pbk.)
  1. Church work with youth. 2. Animated television programs--Moral and ethical
aspects. 3. Animated films--Moral and ethical aspects. I. Title.
  BV4447.C3787 2005
  268'.67--dc22
                                                                    2005002991

Web site addresses listed in this book were current at the time of publication. Please con-
tact Youth Specialties via e-mail (YS@YouthSpecialties.com) to report URLs that are no
longer operational and replacement URLs if available.

Editorial direction by Will Penner
Art direction by Holly Sharp
Editing by Doug Davidson
Proofreading by Janie Wilkerson and Joanne Him
Interior design by Mark Novelli, Imago Media
Cover design by Burnkit
Printed in the United States of America

05 06 07 08 09 10 / DCI / 10 9 8 7 6 5 4 3 2 1

CONTENTS

PART 3: HELPFUL GUIDES

Acknowledgements

Thanks to these resources for some great behind-the-scenes notes:

Animation Insider
www.titanstower.com/animated.html

The Big Cartoon Database
www.bcdb.com

Cartoon Network
www.cartoonnetwork.com

The Simpson1s Archive
www.snpp.com

TV Tome
www.tvtome.com

INTRODUCTION

The apostle Paul said that as we follow God's way we discover that a "basic holiness permeates things" (Galatians 5:22, *The Message*). Does that include a cartoon rabbit and duck arguing over what hunting season it is? You bet it does. Does it include a group of five super-powered teenagers who must stop an evil fish-guy from taking over the world? Actually, yes it does! Does that holiness include a family of yellow people who must survive every day in the town of Springfield? Sure, why not?

Toons That Teach uses your favorite cartoons to dig into that basic holiness that Paul wrote about, to explore our relationships with God and with each other. We'll take classic cartoons from Warner Brothers and Walt Disney as well as modern classics like *Samurai Jack* and the *Powerpuff Girls* and show you how to use them as the basis for biblically-based discussions for junior and senior high kids. You'll find it's an exciting resource for leading your teenagers into a closer relationship with the One who created it all. (No, I don't mean Walt Disney…)

How to Use This Book

This book is a launching pad, not a script. The questions printed here cannot be the only ones asked. No group is the same. You may have more junior high students than the church down the street. Another church may have nearly all girls in their senior high group. No one knows your group better than you do. So think of these questions as a way to get your discussion going.

In each of the 75 lessons in this book, you'll find the following:

SERIES:
The name of the cartoon series (i.e. *The Simpsons*, *Peanuts*, etc.)

EPISODE:
The title of the specific episode of the cartoon.

VOLUME TITLE:
Where you can find the episode on VHS or DVD.

THEMES:
Two or three key topics or issues addressed in the discussion material for this cartoon. Use these themes to choose lessons according to your needs. For example, if you are doing a series on peer pressure, this will help you easily find the cartoons that will work for you.

SCRIPTURES:
Two or three Scripture references (along with a few words about each) that you can use to help make your discussion biblically relevant.

SYNOPSIS:
A brief overview of what happens in the episode.

TOON TRIVIA:
A fun fact you can share with your group. Read these from the book—or memorize and share them to make yourself look like an expert!

OPTIONAL EXTRA:
A suggestion or two for fun activities, games, or snacks that will help make the event more enjoyable.

DISCUSSION QUESTIONS:
You can use these basic open-ended questions to start your discussion out right.

CLOSING PRAYER:
A simple, spoken prayer is provided based on one or more topics arising from the clip. Feel free to have a teen read it to close the discussion, or incorporate it into a prayer of your own.

The Table of Contents lists the lessons by cartoon series and episode title. You'll see that the cartoons are divided into "classic cartoons" and "current cartoons." At the end of the book, you'll find information about where you can find these cartoons on video or DVD, as well as indexes that group the lessons by Scriptures referenced and themes addressed.

SOME GUIDELINES FOR LEADING DISCUSSIONS

▶ Always watch the cartoon with your students. See what you can spot that fits the discussion. Ask your students what they saw.

▶ Be sure you listen to the answers your teens give. Whenever possible, see if you can ask at least one follow-up question based on the answer given.

▶ Share your thoughts, but try to let your students share their thinking first. Let them know that many of these questions simply ask for their opinions; it's not a matter of being right or wrong.

▶ Some teens may feel that cartoons are just for "little kids." Emphasize that cartoon lessons are for everyone. In fact, much of the humor in cartoons is not intended for children at all. *Looney Tunes* were created to be seen by adults attending movies in the '40s. *The Flintstones* was a prime-time sitcom in the 1960s. *The Simpsons* is full of adult humor. Cartoon writers often incorporate deeper messages, references, and jokes that won't be understood by younger viewers. Encourage your students to look deep and listen hard. You may be surprised at what they find.

PART
ONE

CLASSIC
CARTOONS

SERIES
The Flintstones

EPISODE
The Hot Piano

VOLUME TITLE
The Flintstones: Season One

Themes: Consequences, Decisions

Scriptures:

- Proverbs 3:5-6: Confused? Ask God.
- Matthew 6:33: God in all things makes you fully human in all things.
- Romans 13:11-14: "Hey, over here! Remember Me?"–God

Synopsis:

Fred wants to buy Wilma a gift she has always wanted—a piano. But when Fred buys the gift from a less-than-reputable source, hilarity ensues. Fred and the boys eventually get the piano to Wilma, and the boys sing "Happy Anniversary" to the loving couple.

Discussion Questions:

- When was the last time you tried to take the easy way out? What happened?
- Have you ever heard the phrase "There's no such thing as a free lunch"? What does it mean?
- Do you ever get to a point where you hear a little voice inside your head say, "You know, this is a bad idea"? Do you listen to this voice, or do you ignore it?
- Who do you consult when you make important decisions? What if you are trying to decide about something that might get you in trouble—who do you ask then?
- Have you ever made a bad decision—and then made another bad decision to try to cover the first one up? How'd that work out?

- When could Fred have just 'fessed up and gotten himself out of trouble? Why do you think he didn't want to do that? (Granted, that would have made for a much shorter episode!)

TOON TRIVIA

The "Happy Anniversary" song at the end of this episode is to the tune of "The William Tell Overture"—also known as the theme from *The Lone Ranger.*

- If you were offered a deal where you could get a B on every test without studying, but could never get an A, would you take that deal? Why, or why not?

- Would you rather succeed as part of a team and share the recognition, or succeed as an individual but go unnoticed?

- What were Fred's motives?

- How many chances did Fred have to back out of the deal?

- If you were Barney, would you have quit at some point and said, "Sorry, you're on your own"?

- Would Jesus be singing with the boys, or telling Fred he had to return the piano?

CLOSING PRAYER:

God, sometimes we do things even when we know they will get us in trouble. So many times you put up flashing warnings, but we plow right on through. Protect us when we get stupid, God. Lift us out of the holes we make for ourselves. Amen.

 OPTIONAL EXTRA

The Flintstones was famous for its "stone" puns, so have a pun-off. Break the group into two teams and have players come up one a time and make puns. Each player has five seconds to respond. All puns must have something to do with rocks or stones.

SERIES
THE JETSONS

EPISODE
A DATE WITH JET SCREAMER

VOLUME TITLE
THE JETSONS: THE COMPLETE FIRST SEASON

THEMES: Communication, Dating, Parents

SCRIPTURES:

- Proverbs 2:3-6: Seek wisdom and you will find it.
- 2 Timothy 2:7: Stay with the program. God will show you the answer.
- James 3:9-12: Garbage in = Garbage out.

SYNOPSIS:

Judy enters the "Win a Date with Jet Screamer" contest, but George tries to make sure she doesn't win by substituting her song with Elroy's secret code. Judy wins the big date anyway, and George follows close behind to make sure nothing bad happens.

DISCUSSION QUESTIONS:

- When is someone old enough to date? What are the rules in your family?
- Is there any current celebrity that you would like to date?
- What would you do if your mom or dad followed you on a date?
- Is it hard to communicate with your parents? What's the hardest part?
- What do you think your parents would say is hardest about communicating with you?
- We're actually closer to the Jetsons' reality now than we were when your parents were dating. How have cell-phones changed the dating scene since your parents were kids?
- Have your parents ever told you stories about when they were dating? What they did? Where they went?

- Who puts up the wall that sometimes appears between parents and teens? Was it always there?

- Do your parents talk to you differently now from the way they did when you were a kid? Explain.

- How much do your parents trust you? When was the last time you gave them reason not to trust you? How long did it take to earn that trust back?

- Is George being unreasonable? Is Judy? Would you let your kid go out with Jet Screamer?

- Complete this sentence: The biggest misconception adults have about dating today is...

- Complete this sentence: The biggest thing teenagers don't understand about dating is...

CLOSING PRAYER:

Loving God, we are amazed at the differences between us. Help us understand our parents. Help them understand that we are becoming new creations, changing every day. Help them remember what that is like. Amen.

OPTIONAL EXTRA

Create your own secret code with symbols and letters, and then write out one of the suggested Scripture verses on posterboard in your code. Give your group blank sheets of paper and pencils. The first one to translate and read the verse aloud gets an ice-cream bar.

03

SERIES
LOONEY TUNES

EPISODE
BALLOT BOX BUNNY

VOLUME TITLE
THE GOLDEN COLLECTION

THEMES: Leadership, Politics

SCRIPTURES:

- Daniel 4:31: Kingdoms fall. Governments change.
- Romans 13:1-2: Authority deserves respect.
- 1 Peter 3:15-16: If you don't do anything to get on the cover of a tabloid, you won't end up on the cover of a tabloid.

SYNOPSIS:

Yosemite Sam is running for mayor on an anti-rabbit platform. Bugs decides to throw his hat in the ring and run against Sam. In the end both candidates are beaten by a real dark horse candidate.

DISCUSSION QUESTIONS:

- Do you consider yourself a Democrat, a Republican, or neither?
- Do you think voters are treated as if they are stupid during an election year? Explain.
- In one recent election, voters were "selling" their votes on eBay. Do you think this is right?
- How do politicians "buy" votes today? (Cigars not included.)
- Does your youth group have elected officers? Does your church? How are those elections held?
- Is holding an election for church leaders biblical? What elections do you know of in the Scriptures?

- Do you think politics is an honorable profession? Would you ever want to hold public office for a living?

- What issues in your community, nation, or world are you most concerned about?

- Why do candidates spend so much time trying to be "of the people"? (Kissing babies, being "folksy.") Aren't voters smart enough to know who's faking?

- When Bugs says "I speak softly…," he's quoting a famous U.S. president. What do you think that statement means? Is it a good policy for a nation to follow? What about for an individual?

- The sign in Bugs Bunny's office says "Loyal, Loveable, and Literate." What qualities do you look for in a leader? (Bonus point if you name a quality that starts with "L.")

- What is a "dark horse"?

  (A dark horse is a candidate who is relatively unknown or wins unexpectedly. The phrase came from the practice of painting a racehorse so that it would receive better odds.)

- What qualities do the Scriptures tell us to look for in a leader?

- Are you a leader? What kind of leader are you?

- (Optional Question) Were you surprised by the way the cartoon ended? Was this too violent? This was one reason some *Looney Tunes* were edited in the 1980s. Do you think any kids' cartoon today would end with Russian Roulette? Why, or why not?

CLOSING PRAYER:

God, make us leaders. Guide the leaders of our church, our nation, and our world. Make them wise. Give them ears to hear the people and honor to earn their trust. Amen.

 OPTIONAL EXTRA

Hold an election within your youth group, not for leader of the group but for something silly, like Snack Time: Oreos or Chips Ahoy. Have two of your more vocal students square off in a debate. Allow the rest of your group to ask the questions. Hold an election and buy the winning treats for the next meeting.

04

SERIES
LOONEY TUNES

EPISODE
BIG HOUSE BUGS

VOLUME TITLE
THE GOLDEN COLLECTION

THEMES: Crime and Punishment, Justice

SCRIPTURES:

- Job 34:11: We get what we deserve.
- Psalm 37: To God, the bad guys are a joke.
- Jeremiah 17:10: God sees a person's heart.

SYNOPSIS:

Bugs tries to get away from some hunters, but accidentally tunnels into Sing Song prison. There, he is mistaken for a real inmate by prison guard Sam.

DISCUSSION QUESTIONS:

▷ When was the last time you were grounded? Did you deserve it?

▷ What should the punishment be for the following "crimes"?

- A bad report card
- Getting detention at school
- A fender bender in mom's car
- Punching a sibling
- Lying to dad

▷ If you are grounded, should you be able to get shorten your "sentence" through good behavior?

▷ Have you ever been punished for something you didn't do?

▷ Have you ever done something bad without getting punished? Was someone else punished for what you did?

- How does the punishment system work at your house? What about at your school?

- Did you get spanked as a kid? Is there anything wrong with that? If you have kids, do you plan to spank them if they misbehave?

- Does God punish us for the bad things we do? Now, or later?

- If God is love and the Bible says "love does not keep a record of wrongs," does that mean we have a "get into heaven free" card?

- How would you rate the criminal justice system in our country today?

- How would you apply "three strikes, you're out" at school?

- What is atonement? Why does it matter?

TOON TRIVIA

Many of the recent video releases of this particular cartoon have edited out the scene where Sam accidentally hangs himself.

CLOSING PRAYER:

God, we mess things up on a pretty regular basis. Please do not hold it against us. We really are trying most of the time. We will try again, God. Help us learn from our mistakes. Help us seek justice. Amen.

 OPTIONAL EXTRA

Here's a nice affirmation game. Get yourself a plastic police badge. (Most supermarkets have these in their toy section.) Print up phony tickets with each of your kids' names on it. One by one, "arrest" the kids and put them in "jail." To pay the bail for each kid, the rest of the group must say three nice things about that person. To avoid embarrassment. have some back-up "bail statements" in mind before you begin.

05

SERIES
LOONEY TUNES

EPISODE
BIG TOP BUNNY

VOLUME TITLE
THE GOLDEN COLLECTION

THEMES: Ego, Getting Along, Self-confidence

SCRIPTURES:

- Jeremiah 9:23: Even if you are that cool, you don't have to talk about it all the time.
- 1 Corinthians 5:6: Arrogance grows—like a weed.
- 1 Thessalonians 5:14: If others fall, help them up. (This is figurative *and* literal.)

SYNOPSIS:

Bugs Bunny gets a job in a circus performing with Bruno the Bear. Bruno is somewhat unwilling to share the spotlight and tries to "persuade" Bugs to find another line of work.

DISCUSSION QUESTIONS:

- Would you rather work by yourself or as part of a team?
- Do you think the belief that you are better than others is a fundamental human trait?
- Who is the most humble (non-egotistical) person you know?
- Isn't ego a good thing? Doesn't self-confidence work to our favor in the world?
- When does ego get in the way? Explain.
- Have you ever been taken down a few pegs because of your ego? What happened?

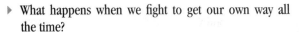

- What happens when we fight to get our own way all the time?

- Daffy Duck is often seen as the *Looney Tunes* character with the biggest ego. Does Bugs Bunny have an ego problem? Explain.

- Are there situations in which too much self-confidence becomes detrimental? Describe such a case. How much self-confidence is too much?

- Read the verses from Thessalonians. How might the ideas from these verses have been worked into the cartoon? How can we reach out to those who think too highly of themselves?

CLOSING PRAYER:

God, we are sometimes so full of ourselves. Help us see that when we think only of ourselves, we wind up pushing aside those we love—we push aside your children. Help us see that our actions have consequences. Show us how to live, God. Let all of us be parts of the body of Christ without always thinking we are the most important. Amen.

 OPTIONAL EXTRA

On a soft carpeted surface, see how high you can stack your students in a human pyramid.

o6

SERIES
LOONEY TUNES

EPISODE
BUGS BUNNY AND THE THREE BEARS

VOLUME TITLE
THE GOLDEN COLLECTION

THEMES: Family, Parents

SCRIPTURES:

- Psalm 133: Life is good when families get along.
- 2 Corinthians 6:11-13: Live bigger.
- Ephesians 6:1-4: Families! Shut up and listen!

SYNOPSIS:

The three bears skip their traditional porridge and cook carrot soup instead, hoping to lure some meat to their house—in this case, Bugs Bunny. Bugs sweet-talks Mama Bear into saving his life, but that creates a whole new set of problems. (Look for the brief shot of Mama Bear in a see-through negligee.)

DISCUSSION QUESTIONS:

- How do you think families have changed since the 1940s when this cartoon was made?
- How many "traditional" families do you know? (By traditional, I mean families with a dad, a mom, and one or more children, where both parents have been married only once.) How many of your friends live in a house with siblings from other marriages? How many live with a single parent? Do you have any friends who have gay parents?
- Who should define what a family is?
- What kinds of things does your family do together? What do you wish your family did together more?
- If you could plan a family vacation, where would you want to go?

- Do people have to live together to be a family?

- Name some fictional parents you've seen on TV. How accurately do television shows and movies depict family life? What TV family seems most "real" to you?

- Are you more like your mother or your father? What about your parents—which of their parents is each of them most like?

- Have you ever known someone from an abusive home? (No names, please.) Did the way the Papa Bear hit Baby Bear bother you? Why, or why not?

- What do you think your parents would say is the best part of being a parent? What makes them the most proud when they talk about you?

TOON TRIVIA

Mel Blanc gets sole credit on this cartoon, even though he only did one voice (Bugs Bunny).

CLOSING PRAYER:

God, we don't get to pick the families we are born into. That's a choice that's made for us. Help us understand that you've put us together for a reason. You knew who we were and who we would need before we were even born. Give us patience, love, self-control, compassion, and kindness. We're going to need it. Amen.

OPTIONAL EXTRA

Make porridge using this traditional recipe:
Blend one cup of oatmeal with four cups of buttermilk. Cook slowly over medium heat.
Add half a teaspoon of salt and two tespoons of sugar. Stir just before serving.
Try serving some porridge piping hot and some ice cold.
(Be careful with the hot stuff.)

07

SERIES
LOONEY TUNES

EPISODE
BUNKER HILL BUNNY

VOLUME TITLE
THE GOLDEN COLLECTION

THEMES: Conflict, Peacemaking, War

SCRIPTURES:

- Proverbs 12:20: Words of peace bring true joy.
- Matthew 5:9: God loves the peacemakers.
- James 3:17-18: Plant seeds of peace; sow righteousness and justice.

SYNOPSIS:

It is the end of the war, and Sam and Bugs appear to be the last two soldiers. Sam tries over and over to take the fort, but always winds up getting blasted in one way or another. In the end Sam says, "If you can't beat 'em, join 'em."

DISCUSSION QUESTIONS:

- Why do nations go to war? If there were a global war that came down to two individuals, do you think they would keep fighting?

- Do you know anyone who is currently involved in a war someplace? What's that like for you?

- Would you serve in the military? Why, or why not?

- Could you fight for your country? Your school? Your home?

- After the tragedy of September 11, 2001, military enlistment skyrocketed in the United States. Is there any situation that would compel you to sign up to go to war?

- Does the Bible say "Thou shalt not kill?" or "Thou shalt not murder?" (Look it up in several translations). If God says we are not to kill each other, is there ever a justification for going to war? When do you think war is justified?

- If we are all God's children (yes, even "them"), what do you think God feels when he sees us fight?

- Why doesn't God step in and stop the fighting?

- Is Sam's solution an honorable one? Is it conceivable in our world today?

TOON TRIVIA

If your VCR or DVD player can do a frame-by-frame mode, watch the scene in which Sam throws the bomb. It's funnier in slow motion.

CLOSING PRAYER:

God, we are all your children. We can cherish each other, or we can kill each other—you have given us that choice. Help us accept the awesome responsibility you have granted us, and do what is good and right and just. Amen.

 OPTIONAL EXTRA

Have a paper ball war in your youth room. You'll need lots of newspapers and a masking tape line down the center of the room. (Flags that say "we" and "they" are also a nice touch.) On the word "go," both teams crumple pages of newspaper and throw the wadded up paper balls to fill the other team's side of the room. Play for thirty seconds and then count the number of newspaper balls on each side. The team with the fewest wins. Now play for five minutes. Teams can assign throwers and collectors and can throw back balls that have been thrown on their side.

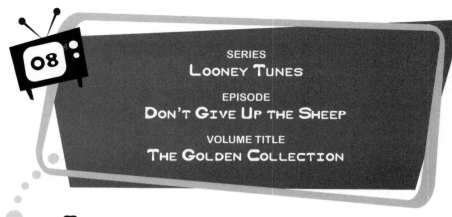

08

SERIES
LOONEY TUNES

EPISODE
DON'T GIVE UP THE SHEEP

VOLUME TITLE
THE GOLDEN COLLECTION

THEMES: Calling, Maturity, Unhappiness, Vocation, Work

SCRIPTURES:

■ Ruth 2:1-13: We must learn to work together.

■ Ecclesiastes 2:18-23: He who dies with the most toys…still dies.

■ Romans 12:20: It's called CHAR-RA-TEEE.

SYNOPSIS:

It's just another day on the job for Sam the sheepdog as Ralf the Wolf tries again and again to score an order of lamb chops and a wool blanket.

DISCUSSION QUESTIONS:

▷ Have you ever worked a job where you had to punch a time clock?

▷ Without considering salary or the education required, what job would you love to do for the rest of your life?

▷ What job you would never want to do?

▷ Workaholism has been called "the respectable addiction." What do you think this means, and is it true?

▷ Sam (the sheepdog) is so focused on his job that he doesn't realize he's being had with the time-clock gag. Would you rather have a job that challenged you and demanded you focus each day, or would you prefer an easier job that allowed you to focus on other things?

▷ If you were a sales representative for Pepsi, could you be friends with someone who worked for Coke? Do you think there are close friendships between Democratic and Republican members of Congress? Explain.

- What is the easiest job in the world? What is the hardest job in the world?
- Could you do a job that asked you to risk your life (police officer, firefighter, circus performer)?
- What is the difference between a job and a calling?
- Do you think you are "called" to do something?

CLOSING PRAYER:

Father God, the world is full of people who are unhappy in their jobs. Help us find our passion. Help us discover what it is that you are calling us to be. Help us find fulfillment, happiness, and purpose in our lives and occupations. Amen.

 OPTIONAL EXTRA

Draw a few cartoon sheep on sheets of paper. (They don't have to be perfect.) Make photocopies and number the sheep from one to one hundred. Then hide the sheep throughout the church building. Separate your group into teams and let them search. The number of points on the sheep is the number of points the team gets. The higher the point value on the sheep, the harder it should be to find.

(Note: Keep a list of where you hide the sheep. I forgot a few and my senior pastor found one in his pulpit on Sunday morning.)

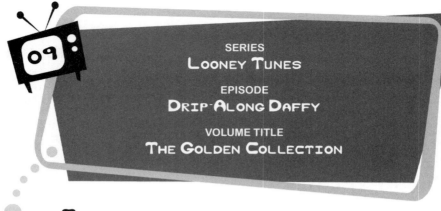

SERIES
LOONEY TUNES

EPISODE
DRIP-ALONG DAFFY

VOLUME TITLE
THE GOLDEN COLLECTION

THEMES: Justice, Maturity

SCRIPTURES:

- Matthew 5:1-12: The Beatitudes.
- Romans 14:12: Rake your own yard before you complain about your neighbor's.
- Philippians 1:27: How do you act when the teacher steps out of the room?

SYNOPSIS:

Daffy and Porky arrive to "clean up" an Old West town. Daffy can't seem to get anything right. In the end, it is the comic relief that saves the day.

DISCUSSION QUESTIONS:

- Have you ever felt like you were life's comic relief? Explain.
- Can you name any classic "second banana" characters? (Examples: Kramer or George, Gracie Allen, Robin, Costello)
- Do you know anyone who acts like Drip-Along—all talk and no action? (No names, please.) What's it like to deal with a person like that?
- What do you think Jesus meant when he said, "The last shall be first and the first shall be last"?
- Read the Beatitudes from Matthew 5. Write a new Beatitude or two based on this cartoon.
- Is life fair? Why does it seem like some people are always getting the fuzzy end of the lollipop?

- What if we don't want to wait for the kingdom of heaven? What if we want to be popular now?
- Which bothers you more—when you are not the one in the spotlight or when "certain other people" are in the spotlight? Explain.
- Would you rather be beautiful or smart? Why?
- Would you rather be "the guy" or "the guy the guy goes to"?

TOON TRIVIA

Look for the Girdle Saloon. At the time the phrase "getting tight" referred to getting drunk. On the "Wanted" poster, Nasty is wanted for the "crime" of calling a square dance. Square-dancing was very big on the Warner Brothers lot at the time.

CLOSING PRAYER:

God, sometimes we want to be the ones standing in the spotlight. We want our moment in the sun. We want center stage. Help us remember that you have a plan for all of us. You have a place for each of us. You have a party waiting that will blow our socks off. Let us be patient, God. Amen.

 OPTIONAL EXTRA

Create your own version of "The Usual" by combining various flavors of sodas, fruit juices, and maybe a little chocolate milk. ("Old Panther" was a term for really bad whiskey. It was originally referred to as "Old Panther Piss.")

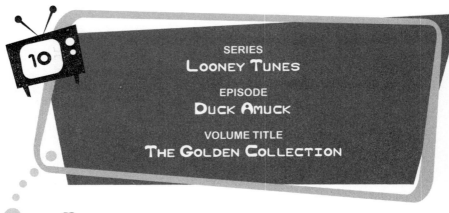

SERIES
LOONEY TUNES

EPISODE
DUCK AMUCK

VOLUME TITLE
THE GOLDEN COLLECTION

THEMES: Anger, God's Will

SCRIPTURES:

- Psalm 16: God is your hero.
- Romans 8:29: God shapes your life into what he needs from you.
- Philippians 2:12-13: Sometimes getting along just takes a little effort on your part.

SYNOPSIS:

A swashbuckling cartoon turns into a free-for-all in which Daffy squares off against an unseen animator.

DISCUSSION QUESTIONS:

- Do you ever feel like there's some unseen force messing around with your life?
- Does God mess with us? Why, or why not?
- Why do bad things happen to good people?
- What do you struggle with most in your life?
- Think about the last time you were "walking through a fire" (so to speak). What helped you come out on the other side? How are you stronger because of the experience?
- Do you know anyone who seems to enjoy making your life miserable? How do you deal with people like that?
- How do you stand up for yourself without losing your temper?

- When was the last time you hit your breaking point? What happened?

- Is there anything wrong with getting angry? Explain.

- What do the Scriptures tell us about struggle? How could we apply this to Daffy's situation?

- There's a famous saying that goes, "We are at our best when things are at their worst." Is this true for most people? Is it true for you? For Daffy?

TOON TRIVIA

Studio executives nearly decided not to make this cartoon, because they felt Bugs Bunny's role was too limited.

CLOSING PRAYER:

God, we know you are there. Sometimes we don't understand why things happen to us, but we know you see what we cannot. You see the big picture. You see what we can become. You see the end result. Help us be patient. Help us be kind. Help us hold on until we become what you want us to become. Amen.

OPTIONAL EXTRA

Find the longest piece of butcher paper you can. If you can find butcher paper, you can use wrapping paper (the white side). Hang the paper on thewall of your youth room so that it streches around the room as far as possible. Use as many colored markers as you can, and have students take turns coming to the paper. The first person can draw anything he or she wants but must leave it incomplete. The second person must start where thefirst person left off and continue the drawing, but the new artist does notnecessarily have to continue the same subject matter. Eventually one drawingwill cover the entire length of paper, and you should have quite an interesting (and funny) mural.

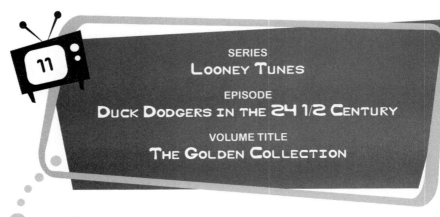

SERIES
LOONEY TUNES

EPISODE
DUCK DODGERS IN THE 24 1/2 CENTURY

VOLUME TITLE
THE GOLDEN COLLECTION

THEMES: Conflict, Ego, Greed, Materialism, Relationships

SCRIPTURES:

- Isaiah 5:20-22: Bad guys lose. Always.
- Ezekiel 22:30: I need a hero!
- Mark 8:35: Put others first.

SYNOPSIS:

Duck Dodgers and his eager young sidekick are sent to Planet X only to find that they are in competition with another explorer from the planet Mars.

DISCUSSION QUESTIONS:

▶ What is the cause of the conflict in this cartoon?

▶ Where does conflict usually come from? Give an example on both a personal and global level.

▶ When Duck Dodgers explains where they are going, he misses the simple idea of following the planets in alphabetical order. Do you know anyone who seems to make everything more complicated?

▶ Why do some people seem happier when the problems are bigger?

▶ Do you think all the problems could have been avoided if Duck Dodgers and Marvin decided to share planet X? Why, or why not?

▶ Can you think of a time when a conflict between you and a friend got way out of hand? (No names, please.) What happened? When Duck Dodgers finally wins the battle and has the planet to himself, what does he really have?

- How can we avoid creating conflict without getting walked on?
- Does "turn the other cheek" mean being a doormat? Explain.

CLOSING PRAYER:

God, we fight over the smallest things. Sometimes we let things that are not really important become be-alls and end-alls because we think we might lose them. Forgive us. Help us loosen our grip on our "toys," God. Help us see the benefits of compromise and sharing, before we lose it all. Amen.

TOON TRIVIA

The Martian in this cartoon is named Marvin, although he is never called by name in this episode or any of the others in which he originally appeared. Creator Chuck Jones said he named the character Marvin because he never knew anyone named Marvin who did anything worthwhile. Also, George Lucas was so enamored by this cartoon when he was younger that when the original Star Wars movie was re-released to theaters, George made sure this cartoon preceded it.

 OPTIONAL EXTRA

Get out a large amount of craft supplies. (You may be able to raid the Vacation Bible School leftovers.) Provide cardboard tubes, paper, glue, pipe cleaners, egg cartons, string, balloons, and anything that sparkles. Have your students create their own bizarro ray guns. Give a prize for the most creative weapon. (Alternately, you might choose for your students to design space costumes, helmets, or other non-weapons.)

SERIES
LOONEY TUNES

EPISODE
THE DUCKSTERS

VOLUME TITLE
THE GOLDEN COLLECTION

THEMES: Justice, Revenge

SCRIPTURES:

- Psalm 106: God will "take care" of those who oppose him.
- Matthew 5:38-42: Return good for evil.
- John 6:37-38: It's all about God's purpose. Not ours.

SYNOPSIS:

Porky appears on a Truth or Consequences type show in which Daffy is the host. The results are disastrous until Porky turns the tables on the host.

DISCUSSION QUESTIONS:

- What is a "glutton for punishment?" (A glutton for punishment refers to someone who keeps making the same costly mistakes over and over without learning from the consequences.)
- Why do some people return to situations they know are harmful to them? For example, why do many women move back in with their abusive husbands?
- Have you ever seen *Fear Factor*? Would you go on that show?
- Is there anything you would never do, even for a million dollars?
- What does the phrase "What goes around comes around" mean? Is it true? Do you have a personal experience? Share it.
- Is there someone you are just waiting for the right time to "pay back"?

- What does the phrase "Revenge is a dish that is best served cold" mean?

- Jesus said, "Turn the other cheek." Should that apply here?

- If Porky were a "Christian pig," wouldn't he just take the money and go home?

- How far should forgiveness extend? Is there anyone you can't forgive? (No names, please.)

- What is the worst thing you have ever done to someone that was forgiven? How about the worst thing you've done that you haven't been forgiven for?

- You've heard the phrase "Forgive and forget." Can you forget without forgiving? What about vice versa?

- On a scale of one to ten, how easy would it be to forgive someone who cut you off in traffic? What about someone who murdered your child? If we are to love as Jesus loves, shouldn't they be the same?

TOON TRIVIA

You might notice that Daffy says "48 States." This cartoon was made before Alaska and Hawaii became states.

CLOSING PRAYER:

God, there are people out there who seem to enjoy hurting us. They take some sort of pleasure in seeing us suffer. You are in charge, God. Not us. Not them. Help us remember that. Help us learn to forgive, so that all might come to know you. Amen.

OPTIONAL EXTRA

Create your own version of Truth or Consequences.
(Don't plan anything too harsh as a "consequence."
A water balloon is probably the most severe consequence you'll need.

13

SERIES
LOONEY TUNES

EPISODE
FAST AND FURRY-OUS

VOLUME TITLE
THE GOLDEN COLLECTION

THEMES: Perseverance, Single-mindedness, Work

SCRIPTURES:

■ Exodus 20:8-11: Even God took a break.

■ Ecclesiastes 4:4-6: Worrying solves nothing.

■ 2 Thessalonians 3:6-18: Everybody works. Everybody eats.

SYNOPSIS:

Wile E. Coyote is hungry and wants to eat Road Runner. (What did you think the synopsis was going to be?)

DISCUSSION QUESTIONS:

▶ All the other Road Runner cartoons were very much like this first cartoon. The producers stuck with the same basic format and plot for every episode. Why do you suppose this is?

▶ Why does Wile E. Coyote want Road Runner? Are there no other options?

▶ What happens when we try to balance all our problems on a single "keystone"? Give an example of when you have seen this happen—either personally or on a bigger scale.

▶ Do you think Americans have become obsessed with work? Why do so many people define themselves by what they do for a living? Is that wrong?

▶ Think about the tunnel that the coyote painted on the wall. Try to come up with a "life hint" about painting our solutions on brick walls. Who does that? What usually happens?

- Do you know anyone who seems to want to run around the road all day having fun?

- How is this cartoon similar to the famous fable of the grasshopper and the ant? What are the similarities? What is different?

- What advice do you think the author of the book of Ecclesiastes would have given the coyote? What would Jesus have told the coyote?

- Is focusing on a goal a good thing? At what point does this become an obsession?

- Are you a roadrunner or a coyote?

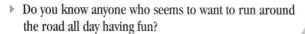

TOON TRIVIA

This is the very first cartoon that features Road Runner and Wile E. Coyote.

CLOSING PRAYER:

God, help us to be less single-minded. There is so much out there in the world. We will accomplish many things with your help, but help us stop and smell the birdseed once in a while. Amen.

 OPTIONAL EXTRA

Split students into pairs and have each pair design a trap that will snare the Road Runner. Have them create blueprints for their traps, using large sheets of blue construction paper and white chalk or wax pencils. Give a prize for the most outlandish idea.

14

SERIES
LOONEY TUNES

EPISODE
FEED THE KITTY

VOLUME TITLE
THE GOLDEN COLLECTION

THEMES: Friendship, Stereotypes

SCRIPTURES:

- Acts 20:35: Think about this: You actually get more by giving.
- Galatians 3:28: Our differences will pull us apart if we let them.
- James 2:8-9: Love others as you love yourself.

SYNOPSIS:

Marc Antony the bulldog makes a new friend in a playful little kitty. Knowing he'll never be allowed to keep it, Marc does all he can to hide his new pet from the lady of the house. Fearing he has lost his friend to a kitchen accident, Marc begins to weep, only to find the story has a happy ending.

DISCUSSION QUESTIONS:

▸ What stereotypes do we put on dogs? cats? teenagers? parents? Christians?

▸ Have you ever held a perception of someone only to find out you were completely wrong? What perceptions do others hold about you that are incorrect?

▸ Have you ever had to explain a friendship to someone? Have you ever had someone say, "I can't believe you're friends with him/her"? How does that feel?

▸ What are the boundaries of friendship? How close a friend do you have to be to help someone with homework? How close to you have to be to ask a friend to help you move? Would you risk your own grade to help a friend cheat?

- Animator Chuck Jones once said that this cartoon was like the complete relationship between a man and a woman in a nutshell. Think about it. Do you agree?

- How can we stop judging people based on their appearances and learn to see what's inside?

- Are there responsibilities that go along with being a friend? Is it fair to have certain expectations of a friendship?

- Have you ever heard the old hymn, "What a Friend We Have in Jesus"? How does this apply here?

- Think about your closest friend. How could you deepen your friendship with that person? What can you do today to make that relationship better?

- Think larger for a moment: What if Marc Antony (the bulldog) represents God, and Pussyfoot (the kitty) represents you? How is this cartoon like your relationship with the Creator?

TOON TRIVIA

Apparently director Chuck Jones wanted the bulldog's expression to be perfect and ordered more than 50 redrawings of the dog's face right after he hid the kitty in the kitchen. (Also, this is the author's personal favorite cartoon of all time.)

CLOSING PRAYER:

God, sometimes we don't know whether to fear you or love you. We get ourselves into all kinds of trouble, and we keep hoping you will bail us out. Pull us back when we stray from the path, God. Hold us close, and remind us that you are our closest friend. Amen.

 OPTIONAL EXTRA

Buy several rolls of sugar-cookie dough and make kitty-shaped cookies for your students. Serve the cookies after the cartoon but before the discussion.

15

SERIES
LOONEY TUNES

EPISODE
FOR SCENT-IMENTAL REASONS

VOLUME TITLE
THE GOLDEN COLLECTION

THEMES: Acceptance, Appearance, Arrogance, Ego, Relationships, Self-image

SCRIPTURES:

- Psalm 145: Take time to thank God.
- Romans 2:1: So how's that whole judgmental thing working out for you?
- James 5:13-16: Prayer is important. Why? Because it works!

SYNOPSIS:

An egotistical French skunk tries to woo a black cat who has had an unfortunate encounter with a bottle of hair dye.

DISCUSSION QUESTIONS:

▸ Of course, this cartoon is meant to make us laugh. But are there ways in which it serves as an illustration of racism at its most basic level? Does prejudice make about as much sense in this context as it does in real life?

▸ Who gets ostracized in your school? (No names, please.) Why does this happen? Has it ever happened to you? What did it feel like?

▸ Both characters have defined movements in this cartoon. Pepé has a distinctive "hop," while the cat seems to be scrambling. How do we "scramble" to get away from our problems? What usually happens?

▸ One of the most entertaining things about Pepé is that he is completely unaware that he is repulsive. Why do some people seem completely unaware of their faults? Do you think this is especially true of people with large egos? Why?

- Can you think of a time when you let your ego get in the way? What happened?

- How do you try to get the attention of someone you want to notice you?

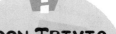

- The cat seemed to like Pepé when he was no longer a skunk, but Pepé wanted nothing to do with the cat when she looked like…well, a wet cat. Are we too caught up in physical appearance? Is this a natural tendency, or is it taught to us?

- Who are the most beautiful people of your generation? What do you think will happen when they get older? What has happened to the beautiful people of your parents' generation?

- How do we become beautiful on the inside? Why does inner beauty seem to matter very little in high school?

- How does God see us? What does the Bible say?

CLOSING PRAYER:

Father in heaven, we don't smell as pretty as we think we do. Forgive us when we let our egos get in the way of our relationship with you. Give us humility by giving us a sense of who you are so that we know who we are dealing with. Amen.

 OPTIONAL EXTRA

Take a favorite hymn or worship song and have your students rework the lyrics with a French accent like Pepé Le Pew's: "Le Jeezuzz he iz ma le sav-YOUR."

SERIES
LOONEY TUNES

EPISODE
HIGH DIVING HARE

VOLUME TITLE
THE GOLDEN COLLECTION

THEMES: Peer Pressure, Risky Behavior

SCRIPTURES:
- Proverbs 3:29-33: Why would you want to be a bully?
- Matthew 14:29: Faith makes a difference.
- Romans 5:2-5: Be smart about it.

SYNOPSIS:
When circus host Bugs Bunny can't produce Fearless Freep the high diver for the audience, Yosemite Sam decides Bugs needs to fill in.

DISCUSSION QUESTIONS:
- ▶ Let's start with one you've all heard before: If all of your friends jumped off a cliff, would you jump too?
- ▶ Why do we indulge in risky behavior?
- ▶ What was the craziest (read: dumbest) thing you ever did? Did you get caught? Did anyone get hurt? Could someone have been hurt?
- ▶ Why do you think adults are shocked by the way some teens behave? Do you think your parents ever did anything crazy when they were teens? Explain.
- ▶ If someone offered you a million dollars to do something, is there anything you would not do?
- ▶ We drive without seatbelts, we speed, we put too many people in our cars—all actions that put us in danger. Why isn't this kind of behavior thought of the same way as something like bungee jumping? Aren't they all risky behaviors?

- Why do we do something over and over again, even when we know we can get hurt? Can you give an example?

- When we indulge in risky behavior, why do we sometimes encourage others to join us?

- Why do people start smoking? take drugs? have unprotected sex?

- What's the strongest kind of peer pressure you face every day?

- Doesn't the Bible call us to live a full life and enjoy the time we spend on earth? Shouldn't we be taking risks all the time?

- What's the difference between risky behavior and stupid behavior? (Note: People called the Wright brothers stupid—they took a risk by flying a plane without insurance or clearance from the tower.)

- Name something risky you would do because the possible payoff is greater than the risk.

TOON TRIVIA

Look for the word Frizby in the opening sequence. This is a nice allusion to the cartoon's director, Fritz Freleng. (Also, you'll want to note how masterful this cartoon is. The whole 'toon is just one joke that's told over and over. There is even one sequence where most of the action is happening off-screen.)

CLOSING PRAYER:

God, sometimes we can take risks that help to make us better people. But be with us when we are doing things that are just plain stupid. Help us know the difference before we act. Help us live in the knowledge that we are yours and to appreciate the life you have given us. Amen.

 OPTIONAL EXTRA

Give each of your students a fairly well-filled water balloon. (Make it bigger than a softball, but smaller than a cantaloupe.) Challenge the students to toss the water balloon in the air to increasing heights. The winner is the one who can toss the balloon highest and still catch it.

SERIES
Looney Tunes

EPISODE
Long-Haired Hare

VOLUME TITLE
The Golden Collection

THEMES: Anger, Conflict, Music, Selfishness

SCRIPTURES:

- Leviticus 9:18: Working for peace isn't always pretty.
- Job 18:5-21: The bad guys lose in the end. Always.
- Romans 12:19-21: Payback is for God, not you.

SYNOPSIS:

An opera singer's practice is interrupted repeatedly by a singing Bugs Bunny. When the singer takes out his frustrations on Bugs, Bugs decides to get even.

DISCUSSION QUESTIONS:

▸ When was the last time you lost your temper? What caused it? What happened later?

▸ How do you deal with conflict?

▸ Read the verses from Romans. What does that passage say about conflict? Is it fair to expect us to live that way in this day and age? Explain.

▸ What happens when we insist on having our own way all the time?

▸ If one is patient and tolerant, and ten is an atomic bomb, where do you fall on the temper scale?

▸ Who has a quicker temper—guys or girls? What's the difference in how guys and girls fight?

▸ What does it mean to "agree to disagree"? Is that even possible?

CLOSING PRAYER:

God, the Bible says you are slow to anger. Thank you for that. Help us be the same. Family and friends are too important to injure or even lose with a careless word or action. Help us to think, to listen, and to speak respectfully. Help us to be your children. Amen.

TOON TRIVIA

The opera singer's name is Giovanni Jones. He was named after the cartoon's creator, Chuck Jones.

 OPTIONAL EXTRA

After the cartoon, use a stopwatch to have a note-holding contest. Find a pair of earmuffs and some white gloves for the person you have playing "Leopold."

18

SERIES
LOONEY TUNES

EPISODE
MY BUNNY LIES OVER THE OCEAN

VOLUME TITLE
THE GOLDEN COLLECTION

THEMES: Competitiveness, Respect, Sports

SCRIPTURES:

- Mark 10:31: The last guy across the finish line is the winner.
- Galatians 6:2-6: Guess who's responsible for who you are? YOU!
- Hebrews 12:14-16: Look out for one another.

SYNOPSIS:

Bugs Bunny makes a wrong turn on his way to Los Angeles and winds up in Scotland. After an encounter with a Scotsman playing the bagpipes, Bugs finds himself in a winner-take-all match of golf.

DISCUSSION QUESTIONS:

▸ How competitive are you? Okay, now, how competitive would other people say you are?

▸ Do you play a game to win, or to enjoy the game?

▸ True or False: "Winning isn't everything."

▸ Is our culture too fixated on winning? Explain.

▸ Do you think most team rivalries are created by the players or the fans?

▸ Even in the Olympics, where the world's greatest athletes compete, the TV coverage still seems to want to have a villain and a hero. Why do you suppose that is?

▸ Have you ever overturned the game board and walked out of the room? Have you ever taken your ball and gone home?

- What is sportsmanship? Can you win graciously as well as lose graciously? How?

- How does that whole last-shall-be-first thing work in football or baseball? Does it work in life?

- Do you know anyone who always seems to have to "one-up" the next person? (No names, please.) How do you deal with people like that?

- How can we learn to stop focusing on destroying our opponents and instead just enjoy the game?

TOON TRIVIA

Half of the humor in this episode comes from the reaction shots. Pay close attention to the close-ups of both characters. Also, notice that there are a number of Scottish jokes. You might want to mention the fact that this cartoon was created years ago, before such jokes were considered unacceptable.

CLOSING PRAYER:

God, we are all players in the game. Help us treat each other with respect and honor. Make us work together so that we can all get better at this game called life. Amen.

 OPTIONAL EXTRA

Set up a miniature golf course in the church hallway. If you don't have clubs and golf balls, you can use rolled up newspapers and balloons. (A penny in the balloon will give it some extra weight. Make the eighteenth hole the senior pastor's desk.

SERIES
LOONEY TUNES

EPISODE
RABBIT SEASONING

VOLUME TITLE
THE GOLDEN COLLECTION

THEMES: Anger, Conflict

SCRIPTURES:

- Proverbs 15:1: Do your words make things better—or worse?
- Galatians 5:22-23: How to stop an argument.
- James 4:1-6: Daddy, where do arguments come from?

SYNOPSIS:

Elmer Fudd goes hunting. Daffy Duck and Bugs Bunny argue over whether it's duck season or rabbit season. Daffy gets his beak blown off several times.

DISCUSSION QUESTIONS:

- Whom do you argue with most?
- Who usually wins?
- When you get into an argument, do you find yourself trying to win the argument, or find a solution?
- Our legal system is based on a sort of "organized" arguing. Is there a right way to disagree? Does it happen?
- What is one good thing that has come out of a disagreement or argument that you have had?
- Imagine that each argument leaves a bruise the same way a fist would. How easily do you bruise? Do your bruises heal, or simply scab over and scar?
- Have you ever stood and watched two people argue, as Elmer does in this cartoon? Talk about that. What happened? How does it feel if they are arguing about something that affects you significantly?

- How is it different if their argument does not concern you?
- Have you ever argued with someone who was really good at arguing?
- Look at the Scriptures. What does the Bible tell us about arguments?
- Do you think it is okay to argue with God? Explain.

CLOSING PRAYER:

God, shut our mouths. We need to hear. Open our eyes. We need to see. Help us hear what we are saying to each other, and what you are saying to us. If we don't learn to listen, somebody is going to lose a beak. Amen.

 OPTIONAL EXTRA

Make a series of paper "ducks" and tape them to the edge of that record player collecting dust in the equipment room. If you don't have a record player, tape the ducks to the edge of a table. Each duck has a point value. Split your kids into two teams and hand them a bag of rubber bands. The team with the highest score wins.

SERIES
LOONEY TUNES

EPISODE
SCAREDY CAT

VOLUME TITLE
THE GOLDEN COLLECTION

THEMES: Confession, Courage, Fear, Listening

SCRIPTURES:

- Psalm 23: Comfort in times of fear.
- Proverbs 29:25: Who cares what others think?
- Mark 4:35-41: Jesus Christ, Demon Slayer!

SYNOPSIS:

Porky Pig and a silent Sylvester move into their new home, only to find that it is already occupied by quite a few territorial mice. Sylvester tries over and over to save Porky's life but winds up getting blamed for everything.

DISCUSSION QUESTIONS:

▸ What scares you the most? When in life were you most scared?

▸ Was the sight of a naked Porky Pig just a little bit disturbing?

▸ What's the difference between being scared by a movie or roller coaster and being scared by a near-fatal car accident? When does it become difficult to distinguish between a "fun scare" and a "real scare"?

▸ The mice aren't after Sylvester. Why is he scared?

▸ Where does Sylvester get his courage? Where does your courage come from?

▸ What was the little blue angel?

▸ Who is your little blue angel?

▸ When is fear healthy? When does it become a problem?

▸ Even with all the "Fear not" Scriptures, sometimes we are still scared out of our pants. How do you think God respond to this?

- Have you ever seen the "No Fear" slogan on T-shirts and skateboards? Is this a healthy motto to live by? Why, or why not?

- How did your parents respond when you were scared as a child?

- How have the things that scare you changed over the years? Are you still afraid of the same things that scared you when you were younger?

- Do you think God ever holds us in his arms and says, "It's okay. It's okay"? Is that how God works? Explain.

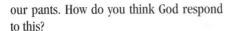

Toon Trivia

This cartoon marks the first time that Sylvester is named as well as the first time that Sylvester appeared in a cartoon directed by the master, Chuck Jones. Jones ran the Warner Brothers animation department for years and was responsible for the creation of some of the most beloved Looney Tunes characters. Also, note that Sylvester is silent in this episode.

Closing Prayer:

God, you are beside us, above us, beneath us, and all around us. Still, we sometimes turn into scaredy cats. Help us be brave. Help us use this natural emotion you have given us so that we can become more like you want us to be. Make us brave, God. Amen.

 OPTIONAL EXTRA

Here's a game called "Cat and Mouse." You will need two balls of different sizes—a golf ball (mouse) and a softball (cat) work nicely. Stand your group in a circle and tell them the object of the game is for the cat to catch the mouse. The mouse can only be passed around the circle in either direction. The cat can only be passed across the circle by tossing it. The object is for the person holding the "cat" to tag the person holding the "mouse." (If you happen to have stuffed animals of the cat and mouse, you can use them to add a little reality to the mix.)

21

SERIES
LOONEY TUNES

EPISODE
TWEETY'S SOS

VOLUME TITLE
THE GOLDEN COLLECTION

THEMES: Getting Along, Relationships

SCRIPTURES:

- Psalm 34: God is like heart glue.
- Ephesians 4:25-5:10: No more lies.
- James 2:12-13: Live a good life, and you'll live a good life. (Yeah, it's that simple.)

SYNOPSIS:

Sylvester the cat stows away aboard a steamship to make a meal out of the little yellow bird he saw from the dock. Fighting seasickness and an old lady with an umbrella (Granny), Sylvester becomes the center attraction in the ship's fireworks display.

DISCUSSION QUESTIONS:

▹ Have you ever tried to play peacemaker between arguing friends? Talk about it. (No names, please.)

▹ Is it possible to dislike someone the very first time you meet? Are some people just natural enemies?

▹ How do we justify bad behavior? ("It's human nature." "The Devil made me do it." "I couldn't help it.") At what point do we need to take responsibility for our own behavior?

▹ How can you help resolve an argument without taking sides? What happens when you do?

- How do men argue differently from women?

- If Tweety and Sylvester decided to work together, would there still be a cartoon? Would it be funny? (Note: This was one of the many original Sylvester and Tweety cartoons, all of which had the same basic plot. Years later, there was a new series, *Sylvester and Tweety Mysteries*, that weren't at all funny.)

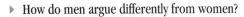

- Sylvester keeps doing the same thing over and over even though it hurts. Is that determination or stupidity? Have you ever done that? What about in your case—was it determination or stupidity?

- Imagine the cartoon reset in a biblical context. Do you think God would protect Tweety from his enemy, or would God help Sylvester achieve his goal?

- What good comes from conflict?

CLOSING PRAYER:

God, we have enemies. We have people who want to see us come to harm. Protect us, God. Give us a chance to reach out to our enemies. Show them another way. Send a peacemaker to bring together those who are at odds. Help us see that we are not so different after all. Amen.

 OPTIONAL EXTRA

Serve "sufferin' succotash" as a snack. Don't serve the vegetable version—instead, invent your own "sufferin'" version by mixing yellow peanut M & M's and green plain ones with bite-size strips of red licorice. You can play around with this "recipe" and see what you can come up with.

22

SERIES
LOONEY TUNES

EPISODE
WHAT'S UP DOC?

VOLUME TITLE
THE GOLDEN COLLECTION

THEMES: Arrogance, Gifts, Growing Up, Loneliness, Self-esteem

SCRIPTURES:

- Psalm 71: Selfish pride can prevent you from getting God's help.
- Romans 5:1-11: Don't take life as it comes. Make it as it comes.
- 2 Corinthians 1:3-4: God is there in hard times too.

SYNOPSIS:

Bugs Bunny tells the story of how he became a big star. First, he's discovered by Elmer Fudd and forced to play second banana. Fed up, Bugs finally steps out into the spotlight.

DISCUSSION QUESTIONS:

▸ List the roles that you play in your life (sister, brother, student, employee #1245). Which role is the most "you"? Are any of them really "you"? Are all of them "you"?

▸ Have you ever been in someone else's shadow? Do you know anyone who has spent their life in someone else's shadow? (No names, please.) What is it like to be near someone who always seems to excel at everything without breaking a sweat? Talk about it.

▸ When does "grown up" begin?

▸ When do you think you will be able to "step out into the spotlight"?

▸ Have you ever been lumped in with a group or assumed to be "just like" someone else? Why do we tend to define people by the groups they hang out with?

- Have you ever been on the receiving end of someone's continuous put-downs? At what point do you say "enough"?

- How do you find the courage to step out onto life's stage on your own?

- Does God give us all gifts? How do you know what your gifts are?

- Someone once said, "Whenever you are doing the one thing that makes you feel most alive, that is where God is." If this is true, when are you "with God"?

CLOSING PRAYER:

God, shadows can be lonely places. Help us realize that you have given us gifts, and you have invited us to step into the spotlight and use them. Help us become what it is you want us to be. Let us use your gifts to us and share them with others. Amen.

OPTIONAL EXTRA

Find and print out a copy of the classic Abbott and Costello skit, "Who's On First." Hand it off to a couple of your biggest hams the week before you teach this lesson, and ask them to perform it for the group. Script can be found here: http://www.psu.edu/dept/inart10_110/inart10/whos.html

23

SERIES
PEANUTS

EPISODE
A CHARLIE BROWN CHRISTMAS

VOLUME TITLE
THE HOLIDAY COLLECTION

THEMES: Christmas, Faith, Holidays, Love

SCRIPTURES:

- Matthew 5:3-10: The kid who used to get his lunch money stolen is going to get the really, really good cookies. No charge.
- Luke 19:10: The lost will be found.
- 1 John 4:7-8: God is love. Look around.

SYNOPSIS:

Charlie Brown searches for the true meaning of Christmas. He looks to his dog, his school play, his "therapist," and his best friend, Linus. It finally takes a little tree and a miracle to put him back in the Christmas spirit.

DISCUSSION QUESTIONS:

- What is the greatest Christmas present you ever got?
- What was the greatest Christmas present you got that was not a material thing?
- What was the thing you always wanted but didn't get?
- What makes a tradition? Does your family have any goofy Christmas traditions that exist only in your house?
- This show was talking about the commercialization of Christmas back when it was made in 1964. Are things better or worse now? Explain.
- Have we lost something as our society has become more high-tech? Explain.
- Have you ever been in a Christmas pageant? Talk about it.

- Why does it seem like there are more Lucys than there are Charlie Browns in this world?

- Look at the scene in the school again. Which kid's dancing resembles the way you look at life?

- This show features cheap animation even for 1964, yet it still does well in the ratings every year. Why is that?

- Why do you think the creators of the show used the song "Hark! The Herald Angels Sing" instead of the obvious choice of "O, Christmas Tree"?

- Charlie Brown didn't get a miracle until he was about as sad as he could be. Does it ever seem like God waits until we are as far down in the hole as we can get before he gives us a rope? Why do you think that is?

TOON TRIVIA

Believe it or not, this show was not aired when it was created in 1964 because it could not get a sponsor. It aired the following year with the words "Merry Christmas from your local bottlers of Coca Cola" on the last screen.

CLOSING PRAYER:

God, you gave us your son so we would finally get the point. You love us. You love us during our Lucy moments and our Charlie Brown moments. Let us celebrate that love. Let us dance like Snoopy. Amen.

 OPTIONAL EXTRA

Show this episode in the middle of summer. Crank down the AC. Serve hot cocoa and peppermint sticks. Have an indoor snowball fight with copy paper snowballs.

24

SERIES
PEANUTS

EPISODE
IT'S THE GREAT PUMPKIN, CHARLIE BROWN

VOLUME TITLE
THE HOLIDAY COLLECTION

THEMES: Faith, Halloween, Holidays, Self-acceptance

SCRIPTURES:

- Psalm 8: Everything is because of God.
- Jeremiah 29:11: Don't worry. God will look after you.
- Matthew 5:13-16: You must be life's flavor.

SYNOPSIS:

The adventures of the Peanuts gang at Halloween. Linus sits in the pumpkin patch with Sally. Charlie Brown gets a little carried away with the scissors. And Snoopy dances, because that's what Snoopy does.

DISCUSSION QUESTIONS:

- Did you believe in ghosts when you were a kid? Did you believe in The Great Pumpkin?
- What was the best Halloween costume you ever wore? What was the best Halloween treat you ever got?
- Why does Lucy pull the football away? Why does Charlie Brown keep trying to kick it?
- What is optimism? When does optimism become foolishness?
- Have you ever been a "Charlie Brown"—gotten carried away with the scissors, been drawn on, had the football pulled away when you went to kick it? Explain.
- Where does Linus spend his Halloween? Does he get to see The Great Pumpkin? Why does he vow to go back next year?

- How old were you when you stopped believing in the old guy in the red suit with the beard? (No, not Satan.) Even if you've seen this before, isn't there just one small piece of you that wants The Great Pumpkin to rise up in the patch? What do we call this "one small piece"?

- Which member of the Peanuts gang is most like you?

- The Scriptures tell us that faith is "the proof of things hoped for and the evidence of things unseen." Do you think this is true? Who has the most faith in this show?

- How do you find the strength to get up and try something again, even when you've just failed at it? How do you find the strength to do something, even though you know it's going to hurt?

CLOSING PRAYER:

Great God, give us the faith of a child in the pumpkin patch. Give us the innocence that brings hope. Give us the eyes of a child, so that we may see the world as a hopeful place and not a hopeless one. Amen.

OPTIONAL EXTRA

You're probably showing this around Halloween, so set up some classic autumn games. Try a pumpkin-carving contest to see who can create "The Great Pumpkin." You can also serve bite-size candy bars.

SERIES
Scooby Doo

EPISODE
Foul Play at Funland

VOLUME TITLE
Scooby Doo, Where Are You?
The Complete First and Second Seasons

THEMES: Friendship, Teamwork

SCRIPTURES:

- Proverbs 18:24: Friendly advice.

- John 15:13-15: Great friends (it doesn't necessarily mean death).

- Hebrews 10:24: Sometimes you have to work at it.

SYNOPSIS:

Scooby and the gang travel to the amusement park, Funland. When the rides start running by themselves, it seems the park is haunted. Scooby and the others try to solve the mystery.

DISCUSSION QUESTIONS:

▸ Who is your best friend?

▸ Is there a difference between friends and people with the same interests?

▸ How come Scooby and Shaggy always have to go off by themselves?

▸ Come up with Shaggy's definition of a best friend. What would Scooby's be?

▸ If your best friend asked you to lie to help get her out of detention, would you?

▸ What if your best friend asked you to lie to keep him from being arrested?

▸ When was the last time you and your best friend had an argument? Are you still friends?

▸ Who was your best friend when you were a little kid? What friend qualifications do younger kids require? How is that different from what you look for in a friend now? How will that change as you get older?

> Is it easy for you to make friends? Is it easy for you to keep them?

> Which character is most like you?

> Which character would your friends say is most like you?

> Which character is most like your youth minister?

> Imagine that Jesus was a character on the show. Whom would he pair up with to hunt for clues? Do you think Jesus would point out all the clues, or just let the gang find them?

> Do you know the song "What a Friend We Have in Jesus?" Rewrite the lyrics to fit with Scooby Doo.

CLOSING PRAYER:

God of friendship, bless our friends. Keep them close to us and keep us close them. Help us put aside our egos and lift each other up. Let us be together. Let us support one another. Let us love one another. Amen.

 OPTIONAL EXTRA

Let your group make individual pizzas, but have some truly bizarre choices for toppings. Peanuts, jelly beans, fish sticks, scrambled eggs, pineapple—be creative. Cook the pizzas while the students watch the cartoon and then eat while you discuss.

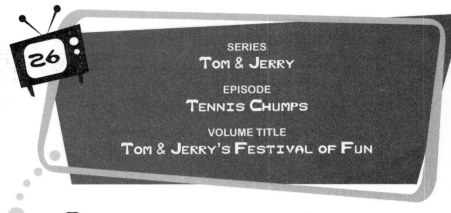

26

SERIES
TOM & JERRY

EPISODE
TENNIS CHUMPS

VOLUME TITLE
TOM & JERRY'S FESTIVAL OF FUN

THEMES: Competitiveness, Winning

SCRIPTURES:

- Matthew 16:26: Don't be a sell-out.
- Mark 9:33-35: You don't have to be first all the time.
- Mark 10:31: Does it bother you that God starts from the back of the line?

SYNOPSIS:

Tom plays Butch in a tennis match. Tom can't seem to win. Jerry eventually winds up playing against both cats.

DISCUSSION QUESTIONS:

- Have you ever felt like someone else is always better than you, no matter what you do? Talk about that.
- In what ways do you tend to measure yourself against others? Grades? Abilities? Looks? Why do you think we tend to compare ourselves with other people?
- Have you ever known someone who puts winning the game above all else? What was it like to play a game with this person?
- Which is more important in a game: having fun or winning? Explain.
- Consider the phrase "It's not whether you win or lose, it's how you play the game." True or false? Back up your answer.
- Can a person be too competitive? Explain. Have you ever experienced such a situation?
- Define sportsmanship.

- When is competition a good thing? How has it helped you?

- In some martial arts competitions, those competing must bow and thank their opponents for the experience. How do you think this would affect your high school football game?

- On a scale of one to ten where one equals "win at all costs" and ten equals "just have fun," where would you place yourself?

- Have you ever known someone who would play both sides just so he could be a winner?

- Have you ever known a person who would "turn the board over" because she was losing?

- Apply the previous two questions to the bigger picture. What kinds of people turn the board over in life? What kinds of people play both sides to look good in the end?

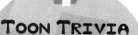

CLOSING PRAYER:

God, we are all winners. Help us act like it. Help us lose graciously and win graciously. We are all your children. Help us keep our tempers and grow from our losses. Amen.

 OPTIONAL EXTRA

Invite your youth to play a non-competitive game that doesn't require winning to have fun. If your church has a ping-pong table, start the meeting by playing a few rounds with crazy rules: each player must stand on one foot, each player must use the non-dominant hand. See if you can play the game with six or eight people per side who must take turns hitting the ball. Finally, play a game with four people, but make the individual players switch sides of the table in the midst of the game so they switch partners frequently. This takes away the motivation to "win at all costs" and helps the youth to focus on having fun as the most important part of the game.

27

SERIES
TOM & JERRY

EPISODE
TRUCE HURTS

VOLUME TITLE
TOM & JERRY'S FESTIVAL OF FUN

THEMES: Being Yourself, Change, Conflict, Violence

SCRIPTURES:

- Matthew 5:9: God loves a peacemaker.
- Philippians 3:1-14: Sometimes you have to be the grown-up.
- James 3:13-17: Don't just talk the talk. Walk the walk.

SYNOPSIS:

Tom, Jerry, and Butch (the bulldog) sign a truce to live peacefully. Things go fine for a while, but selfishness eventually rears its ugly head—and they end up right back where they started.

DISCUSSION QUESTIONS:

- How do fights usually start? How do they usually end?
- Can a tiger ever "change his stripes"? In other words, are we simply born as we are with no ability to change?
- Why is hard to change? When is it hard to change?
- Why do you think there are so many jokes about churches' inability to change? (For example—Question: How many church committee members does it take to change a light bulb? Answer: CHANGE??)
- Is it part of our nature to disagree? Are we naturally programmed to fight? Is it part of being human?
- What agreements have you made that you later found were hard to live up to? Why were they difficult?

- Is there such a thing as "cheating just a little"?
- Tom, Jerry, and Butch seemed to get along just fine for a while. What happened?
- What if Tom, Jerry, and Butch were high school students? What if they were representatives of countries?
- Do nations play Tug of War?
- What relationships do you have that work this way?
- Do you find sharing difficult? Why, or why not?
- What does Scripture tell us about getting along? What would happen if you applied biblical principles to even the smallest conflicts?

TOON TRIVIA

Listen for music from
The Wizard of Oz.

CLOSING PRAYER:

God, you watch over us. Help us stop hurting each other. Help us open our eyes and see what we are doing to each other when we play at war. We are all your children. Help us treat each other that way. Amen.

 OPTIONAL EXTRA

Have two volunteers stand toe to toe, and give them a silly subject to argue about. Example: The cost of tariffs on edible kittens. After a minute have them switch places and switch sides of the argument. If you are brave, play a second round with an issue of controversy in your school, community, or church.

28

SERIES
WALT DISNEY'S MICKEY MOUSE

EPISODE
RUNAWAY BRAIN

VOLUME TITLE
WALT DISNEY TREASURES:
MICKEY MOUSE IN COLOR, VOLUME 2

THEMES: Behavior, Dating, Relationships

SCRIPTURES:

- Proverbs 4:23: Look after your heart. Be careful to whom you give it.
- 2 Timothy 1:7: If you've got it, flaunt it.
- Titus 2:6-8: Lead by example.

SYNOPSIS:

In an effort to raise some extra cash for Minnie's birthday gift, Mickey sells himself for experimentation. An evil scientist switches Mickey's brain with that of a monster named Julius. Now both Mickey (inside Julius) and Julius (inside Mickey) are after Minnie.

DISCUSSION QUESTIONS:

▸ What is the perfect date for you?

▸ Do guys turn into animals when they get around girls? (If you think "yes," then what do girls turn into around guys?)

▸ Could you date someone who was not of your religion? race? species?

▸ What is "courting"?

▸ Is it always the guy's responsibility to ask and pay for the date?

▸ Guys, where do you learn the way to behave "properly" around girls?

▸ Girls, same question.

▸ Has the expected behavior on a date changed over the years? What was expected when your grandparents were going out? What do you think it will be like for your grandchildren?

- Have you ever been on a computer date? Is that dating?

- Could you go out on a date with someone you'd never met before? Have you ever been on a blind date?

- What happens when teenagers get hormones (other than their parents going crazy)?

- Most people (girls especially) are reaching physical maturity at an earlier age than ever before, yet people are waiting longer to get married. Is it too much to ask young people with raging hormones to be "good and pure and virginal" until they are married?

- A youth minister named Mike Yaconelli once said that teenagers should wear WWJD underwear—that way if they were on a date and things went too far too fast, they'd see those letters and stop what they were doing. Do you think that's reasonable?

- How do we learn self-control? Self-control is listed as one of the "fruits of the spirit" in Galatians 5:22-23. Read through this passage. How do these qualities apply to our relationships with the opposite sex?

CLOSING PRAYER:

God, you made us. You know how maddening it is for us as we go through these years. Help us, God. Calm us when we rage. Lift us up when we are depressed. Make us into the kind of adults that you want us to be. Amen.

OPTIONAL EXTRA

Find a stack of "tropical paradise" postcards and send them to all the students who are not there tonight. Write the cards as if you were on some sort of field trip to the islands, and they missed it! (Sure, they'll figure it out from the postmark, but so what?) Also, serve pineapple and other tropical fruits and drinks.

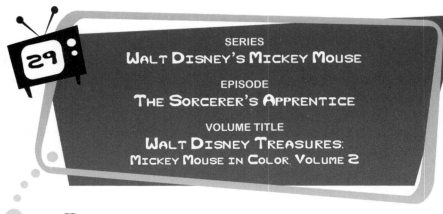

29

SERIES
WALT DISNEY'S MICKEY MOUSE

EPISODE
THE SORCERER'S APPRENTICE

VOLUME TITLE
WALT DISNEY TREASURES:
MICKEY MOUSE IN COLOR, VOLUME 2

THEMES: Career, Maturity, Responsibility, Work

SCRIPTURES:

- Psalm 8: God made us. God loves us.
- Romans 12:3: God blesses us. We say "thank you" by how we live.
- Colossians 3:23: Do everything as if you were doing it for God.

SYNOPSIS:

An apprentice to a sorcerer is left alone with a book of magic and a magic hat. The young apprentice attempts to use the power to do his chores. It doesn't quite go as planned.

DISCUSSION QUESTIONS:

▸ An apprentice is someone who learns a trade by working closely with a person who is an expert in that field. Apprentices work with their "master" until they are ready to take over or go out on their own. Is there any trade in which you would want to work as an apprentice?

▸ Do you think you could survive if you left home right now with nothing but what you could stow in your car? What if you had only what's in your pockets right now? Why, or why not?

▸ Could you have gone to high school when you were seven? Why, or why not?

▸ Who decides when we are ready to face "the real world"? What laws are in place in your state or country that define when people are ready to do certain things (drive, vote, drink, enlist)? On what basis do you think these laws are made?

- In your church, who decides when you are ready to join? Be confirmed? On what basis do we make these rules?

- Fill in this sentence: "_____ is the greatest teacher." (Once they've joked and said your name, lead them toward the word experience.)

- Was Mickey ready to wear the hat? What happened when he tried?

- What happens to us when we try to do something we aren't ready for? Give some examples.

- Do you think anyone knows "everything" about God? Do you think God reveals himself to us a little at a time?

- How could we apprentice ourselves to God? (Not that we can ever take over God's job, but how can learn at the feet of the master?)

CLOSING PRAYER:

God, we want to learn. We want to know all we can, but we aren't ready for the big stuff yet. We may think we are, but sometimes we get ahead of ourselves. Make us ready, God. Teach us what we need to know, when we need to know it. Prepare our hearts so that we will be ready when you decide we are ready to understand what you are about. Amen.

 OPTIONAL EXTRA

Here's a quick and easy mind-reading trick. You leave the room (take a witness if you want). While you are out, a volunteer leads the group in choosing any item in the room. When you come back, the volunteer points to various objects and you "reading their minds" and tell which item is the correct one. The trick: Your "volunteer" is in on the gag. The selected item will be the third item he/she points to after pointing to something black. (You can vary the "code" so that the trick can be done a few times.) As a snack, serve Disney's Magic Cereal (the one with Mickey as the apprentice on the front of the box).

PART TWO

CURRENT CARTOONS

30

SERIES
AQUA TEEN HUNGER FORCE

EPISODE
MAYHEM OF THE MOONINITES

VOLUME TITLE:
**AQUA TEEN HUNGER FORCE,
VOLUME ONE**

THEMES: Behavior, Peer Pressure

SCRIPTURES:

- Romans 12:1-2: Live every part of your life like a child of God.
- 1 Corinthians 15:33: Be careful whom you hang out with.
- Galatians 6:5: Life is a gift. Use it wisely.

SYNOPSIS:

Meatwad's new friends aren't really very good friends. They're disrespectful, they steal, they smoke, and they get Meatwad arrested for shoplifting. It's up to Frylock and Master Shake to help save their friend from a life of hooliganism. *(WARNING: This cartoon is usually shown on Cartoon Network's "Adult Swim" program. The word "frickin'" is used, and one of the moon people seems to flip the bird to the Earth. You may want to watch this episode before showing it to your students.)*

DISCUSSION QUESTIONS:

- Is anyone at your high school like the Mooninites?
- Believe it or not, people like that have always been around. (Remember the bully from *A Christmas Story*?) There were people like that in your grand-parents' day, and there will be in your grandchildren's day. What do you think makes people behave that way? What do you suppose they think they are ac-complishing?
- Err seems to have no other purpose than to follow Ignignokt around and agree with him. Do you know people like this in your school? (No names, please.)

- With all the attention that peer pressure gets in school and church, why does it still have so much power?

- Do you think adults still experience peer pressure? Give an example.

- Frylock and Master Shake don't seem fazed by the Mooninites, but Meatwad suddenly gets arrested and tattooed in order to feel accepted by them. Why do some people go against their better judgment just to be liked by folks they don't even particularly like?

- Whose opinion is most important to you? Why?

- Have you ever changed the way you dress, started listening to a particular band, or used a particular word just to be more like everyone else?

- You've all heard the cliché, "If your friends jumped off a bridge, would you do it?" Take that seriously for a moment. If you had friends who told you how cool it was to jump off a bridge, would you? Doesn't that same logic apply to trying drugs or drinking or stealing?

- Do you think people who behave like Ignignokt and Err really think they are "all that"? Is it possible that this kind of self-confidence is masking something? Have you ever put on a "brave face" so no one would know you were hurting? Explain.

- Is it possible that people like this are just giving out what they are used to getting?

- Is there such a thing as "Christian peer pressure"? How would you define it? Is it good or bad?

- Read the Scriptures. Rewrite Romans 12:1-2 as if Paul were writing the letter to Meatwad.

TOON TRIVIA

The Mooninites are a takeoff on the video game days of old. Most of the sound effects are taken from the Atari 2600 version of Pac-Man.

CLOSING PRAYER

God, we are all Meatwads. Sometimes there is so much out there that we think we want to try, even though we know what the result will be. Give us strength so we can rely on ourselves. Give us friends we can rely on. Help us rely on you as well. Amen.

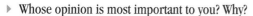 OPTIONAL EXTRA

Spam sculpture contest! Give every student a wad of Spam and allow them to shape it into various sculptures. Bake the sculptures according to directions. Serve with shakes and fries.

SERIES
AQUA TEEN HUNGER FORCE

EPISODE
SUPER BOWL

VOLUME TITLE:
AQUA TEEN HUNGER FORCE, VOLUME TWO

THEMES: Friendship, Popularity

SCRIPTURES:

■ Proverbs 11:14: Listen to smart people.

■ Romans 2:12: There's an honest mistake, and then there's just plain wrong.

■ Philippians 2:12-13: Keep trying. God will give you what you need.

SYNOPSIS:

When Meatwad wins two tickets to the Super Bowl, he suddenly finds he has some new "best friends" who want to share his wealth. Meatwad begins to take advantage of this new popularity and eventually decides to take his new friend Boxy to the game. But did they actually go? *(WARNING: This cartoon is usually shown on Cartoon Network's "Adult Swim" program. Some adult language is used. You may want to view this program before you show it to your students.)*

DISCUSSION QUESTIONS:

▶ Are you popular? Do you want to be?

▶ Is there a "cool kids" table in your school?

▶ What would you do (what have you done) to sit at the cool kids' table?

▶ Why is that so important in high school?

▶ What does it take to be popular?

▶ Have you ever become popular for the wrong reasons?

▶ Have you ever noticed how "friends" come out of the woodwork when you have something they want and disappear just as quickly? Has this ever happened to you?

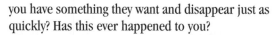
▷ Do you have a friend who would walk ten miles down a hot highway in August just to bring you a cold bottle of water? Is there anyone you would do that for? What are the strengths of a good friendship?

▷ What walls do people put up to keep people from getting too close to them? How do we focus on the good relationships and not the ones that are superficial?

▷ Do you think the same people stay popular after high school? (Ask your youth leader.)

▷ Do you think some companies use people's desires to be popular to promote their products? Name a few.

▷ We have all heard that "God looks at the inside, not the outside." But how does that help us get through a day of school?

CLOSING PRAYER:

God, it is what you think of us that matters. Help us see ourselves as the highest creation of the creator of the universe. Help us see that in others as well. Amen.

 OPTIONAL EXTRA

Fold several paper footballs and divide your group into pairs. Have a football tournament. (Three minutes per game). Play until there are two players left and have the rest of the group watch the paper football "Super Bowl." Serve corn chips as a snack.

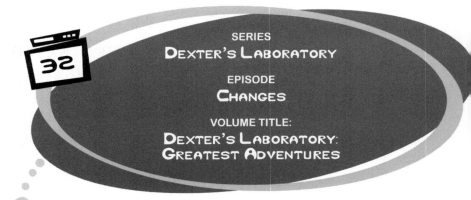

32

SERIES
DEXTER'S LABORATORY

EPISODE
CHANGES

VOLUME TITLE:
**DEXTER'S LABORATORY:
GREATEST ADVENTURES**

THEMES: Appearance, Change, Growing Up

SCRIPTURES:

- Psalm 18: God will protect his own. Ka-Boom.
- 2 Corinthians 5:17: Everyone gets a second chance.
- Philippians 4:11-13: Be satisfied with who you are.

SYNOPSIS:

Dexter and Dee Dee change each other into a number of different creatures with Dexter's new invention.

DISCUSSION QUESTIONS:

- Imagine you have one of Dexter's remotes in your hand and can aim it at yourself and change into any animal. What would it be?
- Let's say you can only change one thing about you physically. What would it be? What if you could change your location? Where would you go?
- Have you ever heard the phrase "The only constant is change"? What does it mean? Is it true?
- Why are some people terrified of change? What was the last big change in your life? What was the last big change in your church?
- What did Jesus say about change? (Read Matthew 3:8.)
- What is risk? How much are you willing to "put yourself out there" and risk getting hurt?

- Do you enter a swimming pool from the shallow end with your toes first, or do you do a cannonball off the diving board?

- What if changes in life happened as quickly as in this cartoon? How would we react? How would life be different?

- What happens when our life changes in ways we don't want it to?

- Would you rather see a big change coming so you can prepare for it, or have the change blindside you and then adjust to it? Which has been your experience?

- Who decides most of the changes in your life? Is that something you wish could change?

TOON TRIVIA

Note that when Dee Dee changes into a bunny, her shadow doesn't change.

CLOSING PRAYER:

God, nothing stays the same very long. Sometimes it seems like we finally get it together, and then it all changes on us. Help us know that there is one constant in our lives: You. You will never leave us. You will never let us alone. You will never let us be stuck for too long. Thank you. Let us feel your presence. Amen.

 OPTIONAL EXTRA

Have your group sit in a circle with one person in the center. The middle person must close his or her eyes as other people in the circle take turns sitting on that person's lap and doing their best impressions of Dexter or Dee Dee. The middle person tries to guess who is sitting on his lap. When the guess is correct, the "sitter" becomes the new middle person, and the game continues.

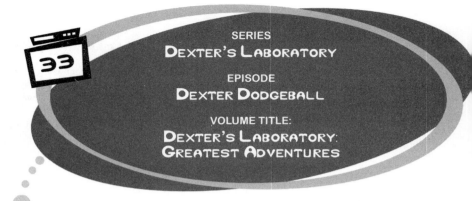

SERIES
DEXTER'S LABORATORY

EPISODE
DEXTER DODGEBALL

VOLUME TITLE:
DEXTER'S LABORATORY:
GREATEST ADVENTURES

33

THEMES: Bullies, Gifts

SCRIPTURES:

- Deuteronomy 9:2-3: You can stand up to bullies.
- Psalm 136: Persistence pays.
- Ecclesiastes 10:10: Nerds win!

SYNOPSIS:

Dexter's written note doesn't cut it with a sadistic new gym teacher, so Dexter is forced to participate in gym class with some larger kids. Dexter creates a robo-suit and shows the big kids how it's done.

DISCUSSION QUESTIONS:

- Have you ever gotten totally creamed in a game of dodgeball—or some other gym-class activity?
- Why do some otherwise normal people get sadistic when you put them in a competitive situation?
- What do you do in situations where you feel like you don't belong?
- What do you do when you walk into a situation that you know from the beginning won't turn out well?
- What did Dexter do about his situation?
- What are your gifts?
- How similar is this gym teacher to the ones you've known?

- Why do some people take such joy in beating up other people?
- If life is a gym class, what do we need to survive?
- If life is a gym class, what would Jesus do?
- Why is it easier to tear others down than to build them up?
- What do we accomplish by making someone else's life more difficult?
- Read Deuteronomy 2:3. Does that sound like the end of a Dexter cartoon?
- Bullies rarely want to fight; they usually just want to bully. How do you find the courage to stand up to a bully?
- What if the bully is a teacher?
- You don't have the option of making a robo-suit. What do you do in situations where you are outnumbered or overmatched?
- Read Matthew 5:2-11. Pick a Beatitude for Dexter.

CLOSING PRAYER:

God, sometimes everybody else is bigger than we are. Sometimes everybody else is better at the game. Sometimes we just get our butts kicked. Help us out here, God. Give us just a little glimpse of the paradise you promised. Give us strength to deal with bullies. Let the gifts you have given us shine. Amen.

 OPTIONAL EXTRA

Glue a batch of green army men to Popsicle sticks. Using a small paper wad (flicked with the finger) you can play table-top dodgeball.

34

SERIES
DEXTER'S LABORATORY

EPISODE
PICTURE DAY

VOLUME TITLE:
**DEXTER'S LABORATORY:
GREATEST ADVENTURES**

THEMES: Appearance, Self-acceptance

SCRIPTURES:

- 1 Samuel 16:7: God has different standards than ours.
- Psalm 139: God is present in all things at all times.
- Proverbs 11:2: Smart people know when to keep their mouths shut.

SYNOPSIS:

Dexter is determined to have a good school picture this year, so he creates a new face. Unfortunately, his plans begin to melt before his eyes.

DISCUSSION QUESTIONS:

▶ Have you ever had a school picture taken that you liked? Has anyone?

▶ Why do we have a tendency to dislike the way we look? By what standard do we judge ourselves?

▶ Is it fair that some people are more physically attractive than others? Why, or why not?

▶ Who do you look like? Who do you wish you looked like?

▶ Have you ever tried to change your "look" (clothes, hair, glasses)?

▶ Have you ever seen a really nice car and compared it to the one you were riding in? Is that normal? Is it natural to see someone on TV or a magazine and wish you looked like that?

▶ Some people say that it's not so much how you look as how you feel about how you look. Is that true? How can we feel better about how we look?

▶ The Scriptures tell us not to look on the outside and not to envy those who are rich and beautiful. Why are those things hard to do?

CLOSING PRAYER:

God, look at us. If we are your favorite creation, then help us see what you see. Help us feel good about who we are and not jealous of others. Help us understand that it is your standards that are important, not the world's. Make us beautiful in your eyes. Amen.

TOON TRIVIA

This episode calls to mind the classic story *The Picture of Dorian Gray*, in which a man doesn't age, but his picture does. The end of that story is similar to Dexter's adventure here.

 OPTIONAL EXTRA

Have each of your students bring in a copy of their worst school picture ever. Then shock them all by showing them yours—or your senior pastor's.

35

SERIES
FUTURAMA

EPISODE
GODFELLAS

VOLUME TITLE:
FUTURAMA, VOLUME 3

THEMES: Faith, God's Will, Image of God

SCRIPTURES:

- Psalm 53: Preach that there is no God, and God will preach there is no you.
- Isaiah 44:6-20: God is God. There is only one. What more do you need?
- Romans 11:34-36: You don't have to understand God to love God.

SYNOPSIS:

Fry and Leela begin searching for God. Bender becomes a god but then finds the real God.

DISCUSSION QUESTIONS:

- How do you search for God?
- How many different names for God can you come up with?
- Do you think all religions basically worship the same God?
- Are you a god to the fish in your fish tank?
- What does Bender learn about being a god?
- What did Fry do for information when the other resources had been exhausted?
- Have you ever read your horoscope in the newspaper? How much stock do you put in those answers?
- Has technology helped or hindered our understanding of God? Explain.
- Could you be God? If you were offered the job for 24 hours, what would you do?

- What do you think is God's greatest accomplishment? What does the Bible say?

- Do you think God gets tired?

- Why doesn't God just bring his big ol' God face down here and say, "See? I do exist!"?

- In this episode God says, "When you do things right, people won't be sure you've done anything at all." What do you think this means? Is it true?

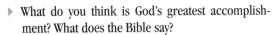

TOON TRIVIA

The coat worn by the priest in this episode bears a striking resemblance to the one worn by Joseph in the film version of *Joseph and the Amazing Technicolor Dreamcoat.*

CLOSING PRAYER:

God, we want to know you. We want to be 100 percent sure that we are not just speaking to the ceiling. Strengthen our faith, God. Help us believe that we don't need proof. It's all very confusing. Help us sort it out—and give us time and patience as we do that. Amen.

 OPTIONAL EXTRA

Do a quick read of Dr. Seuss's *Horton Hears a Who*. You can also order a wide assortment of little green army men from the US Toy Company (www.ustoyco.com) for less than three bucks a gross. Purchase several gross and set them up all over the youth room. See if kids can walk through the room without disturbing the "civilizations."

36

SERIES
JUSTICE LEAGUE UNLIMITED

EPISODE
FOR THE MAN WHO HAS EVERYTHING

VOLUME TITLE:
JOINING FORCES

THEMES: Destiny, The Future, Goals, Life, Predestination

SCRIPTURES:

- Proverbs 19:21: Make plans, but God's plans come first.
- Philippians 2:13: God will give you the strength to do what is right.
- James 4:14: Tomorrow never knows.

SYNOPSIS:

Batman and Wonder Woman go to the Fortress of Solitude to help Superman celebrate his birthday. But the villain Mongul has already given Superman a gift—a plant called "Black Mercy" that gives the victim a very real dream that is difficult to awaken from.

DISCUSSION QUESTIONS:

▶ What if you could experience a perfectly pleasant life with all you ever wanted to be happy—but it wasn't real. Would you stay?

▶ Is there one thing in your past that you wish you could change? If it were possible to go back and change it, would you? Think of all that has happened because of that one event. Would any of those things still happen?

▶ Do you think God has already preplanned everything that's ever going to happen to us? Or do you think God put out some sort of "game board" and gives us the opportunity to make decisions along the way? Does it matter?

▶ Do you think everyone has a destiny? Do some people have a destiny and others don't?

- How might our world be different if the following events had never happened?
  - What if the Continental Congress had been arrested for treason and hanged?
  - What if Rosa Parks had given up her seat?
  - What if the terrorists' plot had been found out before September 11th?
- Looking back at your life so far, when did you grow the most as a person? What were the big changes that made you who you are?
- How much choice do you have in your own future? What is a calling?
- Why do you think the plant was called Black Mercy?
- What does the Bible tell us about our future and our place in the vast scheme of things?

TOON TRIVIA

Look closely at the theater in Batman's flashback. You'll see the movie is *The Mark of Zorro*— a film about an expert fighter who pretends to be a playboy by day and puts on a mask at night to fight bad guys. Hmmmmmm…

CLOSING PRAYER:

Watching God, you get to see the big picture. We hold only one tiny puzzle piece in our hands. We need you to guide us as we go. Help us listen. Help us find a way to be the people you want us to be now, so we can become the people you want us to be later. Amen.

OPTIONAL EXTRA

Have a birthday party for Superman. Most party stores will have little kids' plates, hats, and those little things you blow in that make the paper tube go "whoosh." Bake a cake and do it up right. Be sure to sing "Happy Birthday" to the Man of Steel. Then watch the program.

37

SERIES
KING OF THE HILL

EPISODE
THE COMPANY MAN

VOLUME TITLE:
KING OF THE HILL: SEASON 1

THEMES: Honesty, Integrity, Parents, Stereotypes

SCRIPTURES:

- Luke 8:4-8: Good roots = good crops.
- Philippians 4:8: Be true, noble, and honest—and you will be whole.
- 1 John 5:14-15: Be honest before God, and you will get what you need.

SYNOPSIS:

Hank is forced to take an obnoxious client out for a night on the town while Peggy entertains the client's wife at home. Meanwhile, Bobby must prepare a report for his Sunday school class.

DISCUSSION QUESTIONS:

▸ What would you do to get a contract? How far would you be willing to go?

▸ With that big a contract on the line, is a little white lie justified?

▸ Have you ever changed your wardrobe, speech, or hair to impress someone?

▸ What is something you learned from watching your parents' example? (Be careful, now!)

▸ Has anyone ever made assumptions about you because of where you are from your accent? your gender? How did that feel? Have you ever done this to someone else?

▸ Has anyone ever stopped a conversation or changed their behavior when they discovered you were a Christian?

- What is the greatest stereotype people have about teenagers?

- What is integrity? Is Hank a man of integrity?

- What did you think of the conversation between Hank and Chiffon?

- How do we learn to trust businesses? We assume we're paying for a gallon of gas, but it could be less. We assume we are buying a high quality item, but that might not be true. How does a business earn a reputation for being honest? How does a person earn a good reputation?

- Would you pass up a great job because the manager asked you to lie for him or her?

- Who is your hero? Why?

- Could Jesus be your hero? Explain. What would your classmates do if you read a report in school that said Jesus is your hero?

- Who behaves the most like Jesus in this episode?

TOON TRIVIA

The character of Mrs. Holloway is voiced by Stockard Channing, who also plays the First Lady on NBC's *The West Wing*.

CLOSING PRAYER:

God, we know that you know us. We cannot fool you. You created us. You know us inside and out. Help us live lives worthy of being called your children. Help us to be truthful, even when it's going to hurt. Amen.

 OPTIONAL EXTRA

Hank gets to deal with honesty in this episode, so play an honesty game. Pass out index cards and have everyone write down three things about themselves that no one else will know. Tell them to make one of the statements a lie. See if the rest of the group can spot the lies.

38

SERIES
KING OF THE HILL

EPISODE
HILLOWEEN

VOLUME TITLE:
KING OF THE HILL: SEASON 2

THEMES: Denominations, Faith, Halloween, Holidays

SCRIPTURES:

- Matthew 23:27: You can't be a Christian just because it looks good.
- 1 Corinthians 3:12: A proper foundation will keep you together.
- Hebrews 10:24-25: Don't tear down. Build up.

SYNOPSIS:

Hank and his buddies are outraged when a new woman in the community tries to outlaw Halloween. Bobby becomes worried his father is a Satanist.

DISCUSSION QUESTIONS:

- What is your favorite Halloween memory?
- Do you know the history of All Hallows Eve? (For a quick overview check out *http://www.catholicculture.org/docs/doc_view.cfm?recnum=3169*)
- Conservatives sort of take it on the chin in this episode. Does Junie have a point?
- How has Halloween changed since you were a kid? How has it changed in the last twenty or thirty years? (Ask your youth worker.)
- Are we teaching kids the wrong way to celebrate?
- Why do people get upset about ghosts and ghouls and bite-size Snickers bars?
- Has anyone ever told you that you were going to hell? How old were you? Were you scared? Are you scared now?

- What are some responses the Christian community has come up with for Halloween?
- Have you ever been to a church-sponsored "Hell House" type of event? What was that like?
- What is Bobby afraid of? What is Junie afraid of?
- Is Junie a bully? How do you deal with bullies?
- How do you argue with people who think that they are correct "because God said so"?
- Read the verse from 1 Corinthians. What do you think this says about denominations? Explain. Would you feel comfortable in another denomination?
- Read Matthew 23:27. What does Jesus want Christians to be most concerned about? What would he have to say to the characters in this episode?

TOON TRIVIA

The voice of Junie (the conservative Christian) is Sally Field, who began her TV career as that teenage beach scamp Gidget and later starred as a flying nun in the TV series... well... *The Flying Nun.*

CLOSING PRAYER:

God, we are like kids with plastic trick-or-treat bags. We pray, and we think you will just load us up. Help us remember that we must try to hear, understand, and love one another if we truly want to hear, understand, and love you. Amen.

 OPTIONAL EXTRA

If you show this episode around Halloween, be sure to check out the "Service For All Hallows Eve" in *The Book of Uncommon Prayer* (Youth Specialties, 2000). You could also plan a series of Halloween-like party games. Serve bite-size candies as a snack.

39

SERIES
KING OF THE HILL

EPISODE
REVENGE OF THE LUTEFISK

VOLUME TITLE:
KING OF THE HILL: SEASON 3

THEMES: Forgiveness, Guilt, Honesty, Love, Sacrifice

SCRIPTURES:

- Psalm 103: Life is short. Appreciate it.
- 1 Corinthians 13:5: Love is not selfish.
- 1 John 1:9: Confession is good for the soul.

SYNOPSIS:

As the town prepares to say good-bye to the minister, Bobby eats all of the pastor's lutefisk and then accidentally burns down the church. At first he tries to run away from his shame, but eventually he confesses to both crimes. It is his grandfather who saves the boy from a lifetime of humiliation.

DISCUSSION QUESTIONS:

▷ Should women be pastors? Some churches allow this; others don't. Do you know what your church's stance is and why?

▷ What did you think of Hank's comment that the previous minister was sensitive to afternoon sporting events? Was that sexist? What about the things Cotton said?

▷ Think back to the worst thing you ever did. (Don't say it out loud.) Did you get in trouble? Did you ever tell anyone?

▷ Who does Bobby meet as he's buying a bus ticket to run away from home? If this were real life, would you call this an act of God? Why, or why not?

▷ The minister says, "Jesus forgives you." Do you think Jesus really will forgive anything we do? Are there some things Jesus won't forgive? If we believe that Jesus forgives and forgets, why do we seem to have such a problem doing so?

▶ Is there anything in your past that you still haven't forgiven someone for? (No names, please.) Why not? Do we have a right to hold people's actions over their heads forever?

▶ What is atonement?

▶ How would things have been different if Bobby had not confessed to the police?

▶ Who received grace?

▶ Could you have done what Cotton did at the end?

▶ Who winds up being the most Christ-like in this episode?

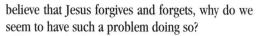

TOON TRIVIA

The guest voice in this episode is Mary Tyler Moore, the famed actress from the television show of the same name.

CLOSING PRAYER:

God, forgive us. Just forgive us, okay? Amen.

 OPTIONAL EXTRA

If at all possible, serve lutefisk. If that's too dangerous, maybe try a tuna casserole that everyone helps to make. You can add a variety of "church casserole" ingredients like crushed potato chips, celery, cream of mushroom soup, and Velveeta cheese. Be creative. Let it cook while you watch the video and serve it up during the discussion.

SERIES
KING OF THE HILL

EPISODE
TO SPANK WITH LOVE

VOLUME TITLE:
KING OF THE HILL: SEASON 3

40

THEMES: Crime and Punishment, Respect, School

SCRIPTURES:

- Deuteronomy 33:20-21: God will bless those who are obedient.
- Proverbs 1:24-30: There is a time for punishment.
- 1 Peter 2:17: It's all about respect.

SYNOPSIS:

Peggy is asked to be a substitute teacher for a Spanish class but is driven to violence by the disrespect of some of the students. Peggy spanks one of the culprits, thereby setting off a town-wide debate. When a news crew shows up, Peggy accuses a neighbor boy of stealing her paddle. She flies into a rage, and then is troubled when she sees a reflection of herself. She returns to the school and tries to remember what it was like when you didn't have to threaten students to get them to pay attention.

DISCUSSION QUESTIONS:

- Did Peggy do anything wrong?
- Is it hard to believe that paddling was once part of daily school life?
- Did you parents ever spank you?
- Is there a high school or adult equivalent to getting a spanking?
- What do your teachers or other adults say about the way things used to be in school as far as discipline goes?
- Do any of your teachers have a "Paddlin' Peggy" type nickname? What is it?

- Which teacher did you hear the most about when you were in a younger grade? Was the reputation deserved?
- Have you ever noticed that the students who seem to dislike a teacher most are the ones who usually give the teacher a hard time?
- What's the biggest punishment a student can receive in your school? Which punishment carries the biggest stigma? Which is the most effective?
- Few schools still use paddling for discipline. Have we gone too far in the other direction? Is there a difference between paddling and being abusive?
- Is fear a good way to encourage better behavior?
- Is the fear of going to hell a good encouragement for Christians to be more Christ-like?
- Did Joseph deserve what he got?
- Who received grace in this episode?

TOON TRIVIA

There's a nice Monty Python reference when Peggy talks about The Spanish Inquisition.

CLOSING PRAYER:

Teaching God, make us listen. You have all these amazing things you want to teach us, and we spend way too much time making noise and cutting up. Focus us. Get our attention. We want to learn. Amen.

 OPTIONAL EXTRA

The Substitute: Substitutes have been harassed by students for as long...well, for as long as there've been substitutes. Have a volunteer at the front play the role of 'substitute' with a ruler. Have the rest of your group begin lobbing paper wads (no saliva, please), and count how many the substitute can swat back.

41

SERIES
PINKY AND THE BRAIN

EPISODE
PAVLOV'S MICE

VOLUME TITLE:
WORLD DOMINATION TOUR

THEMES: Behavior, Decisions

SCRIPTURES:

- Matthew 7:3-5: Examine yourself before focusing on others.
- Matthew 20:1-16: You don't get to decide when.
- James 1:19: Listen more than you speak.

SYNOPSIS:

Pinky and the Brain have been "conditioned" to respond to the sound of bells and gongs. This throws a crimp into Pinky's plan to take over the world by stealing the crown jewels.

DISCUSSION QUESTIONS:

▸ What is conditioned response? Who was Pavlov? *(Pavlov was a scientist who conducted an experiment in which he rang a bell every time he fed his dogs. After a while, the dogs began to salivate whenever he rang the bell. This is conditioned response.)*

▸ Do you believe conditioned response occurs in humans?

▸ Are you conditioned? What about school bells? Music? Sale signs?

▸ Have you ever started salivating when a pizza commercial came on the air?

▸ Who is most responsible for your behavior?

▸ Have you ever heard anyone say, "My mother made me this way."? Is that accurate, or an excuse?

▸ How much willpower do you have?

- What is addiction? Do you have any addictions?
- When was the last time your behavior got you in trouble? What happened?
- How do we break free of "conditioned responses?"
- How does the Bible ask us to behave?
- Do you think that a "Christian conditioned response" exists? Explain.

TOON TRIVIA

Pinky and the Brain was created by film director Steven Spielberg. For a complete list of "Pinky's Ponderings" check out: *http://www.snowball. frogspace.net/labnotes/ aypwips*

CLOSING PRAYER:

God, you have created us with the ability to choose our own paths, our own responses, our own future. Help us see all the options, and fill us with the courage to move forward. Then give just a little confidence and faith that we are doing the right thing. Amen.

OPTIONAL EXTRA

Have an "I'm A Little Teapot" contest. Keep speeding up the tempo. When kids mess up the words or lose their balance, they are out of the game.

42

SERIES
POWERPUFF GIRLS

EPISODE
BUBBLEVICIOUS

VOLUME TITLE:
**BUBBLEVICIOUS (VHS);
POWERPUFF BLUFF (DVD)**

THEMES: Growing Up, Maturity, Parents

SCRIPTURES:

- Psalm 139: We are all the unique creations of a creator God.
- Proverbs 21:5-6: Good things may take time.
- Jeremiah 29:13: If you are willing to work for it, you'll get it.

SYNOPSIS:

Bubbles is tired of being seen as a child by her sisters and the professor. After beating the "Danger Room" on the highest level, she decides to go solo. Though she longs to be "hardcore," she learns that being part of a team is much better.

DISCUSSION QUESTIONS:

- When was the last time someone spoke to you as if you were half your age? Who was it? What did that feel like?
- Why do you think it's so hard for your parents to see you as an adult—or at least as a teenager?
- How did the professor treat Bubbles at the beginning of the episode? How did his attitude change? Why?
- When does "grown up" begin? Legally? In your own mind?
- Do you agree that "mercy is for the weak"? Explain.
- Two sixteen-year-olds go to a party. Both of them are offered a joint. One will turn it down. One will take it. What causes the difference? Where does

that strength come from?

- What's the hardest part about growing up?
- Does maturity happen automatically as we grow older? What causes people to become more mature? Explain.
- What is the most important thing you've ever done on your own?
- Have you ever known someone who wants to be treated as an adult but then turns around and says, "I'm just a kid"? Is it possible to have it both ways?
- Would you rather work alone and get no praise at all or work as part of a team and share the reward?

TOON TRIVIA

The "11" can be seen as a subtle reference to the movie *This Is Spinal Tap*.

CLOSING PRAYER:

Creator God, we sometimes feel like we are stuck in the middle. We want to be seen as adults, but everyone treats us like children. This is a long trip, God. Help us not to lose sight of the fact that we aren't alone. We have friends and family walking with us, and we have you to guide and accompany us on the path. We will be adults soon enough. Help us be your servants. Amen.

OPTIONAL EXTRA

Create your own "Danger Room." Give your group a stack of newspapers and tell them to make as many paper balls as they can. Then youth take turns standing in front of a wall as the rest of the group heaves paper balls at them. The player against the wall gets one point for each paper ball he or she can smack away.

43

SERIES
POWERPUFF GIRLS

EPISODE
CAT MAN DO

VOLUME TITLE:
BUBBLEVICIOUS (VHS);
POWERPUFF BLUFF (DVD)

THEMES: Authority, Decisions

SCRIPTURES:

- Proverbs 18:13-17: If you want to be seen as an adult, you'll have to work at it.

- Romans 13:1-6: Certain responsibilities go along with growing up.

- 1 Corinthians 13:11: There's a time to let go of childish things.

SYNOPSIS:

An evil cat hypnotizes the professor into stealing rare jewels. The jewels are then used to power a machine that brainwashes the townspeople into being the cat's slaves.

DISCUSSION QUESTIONS:

▷ Who made the decisions when you were a child? Who decided what you ate, what you wore, and when you went to bed?

▷ Can you think of a time when you openly defied one of your parents' decisions? How did that go?

▷ Who makes the majority of the decisions about your life now? Who decides what you wear and eat, and when you go to bed?

▷ When does a person officially become an "adult"?

▷ List five people who have authority over you. Would your list have been the same if you'd made it this time last year? How about five years ago? How do you think your list will change in the next five years?

- Have you ever known people who seem content to be led around by the nose, allowing others make all their decisions for them? (Without saying names, talk about that.)

- Have you ever known someone who won't listen to anyone in authority no matter what?

- When is it a good idea to defy authority? When is it a good idea to shut up and get in line?

- Who is the ultimate authority? What are the rules? What did Jesus say were the most important rules?

TOON TRIVIA

The cat and his "owner" are based directly on the primary villain from many of the early James Bond movies, which are also parodied in the Austin Powers films.

CLOSING PRAYER:

God, you are the ultimate authority. Help us know when to put things in your hands and when to use our own. Above all else, God, help us listen. Help us know the difference between good decisions and bad ones. Open our ears. Amen.

 OPTIONAL EXTRA

Make paper bag puppets of the cat from this episode. Have the kids write short skits in which the cat tells them what decisions to make in their own lives.

44

SERIES
POWERPUFF GIRLS

EPISODE
MR. MOJO'S RISING

VOLUME TITLE:
BUBBLEVICIOUS (VHS);
POWERPUFF BLUFF (DVD)

THEMES: Jealousy, Peer Pressure, Relationships

SCRIPTURES:

- Proverbs 17:12-14: Be careful who you hang out with.
- Ecclesiastes 9:11: Eventually can be a very long time.
- Philippians 4:12-13: Learn to appreciate what you have.

SYNOPSIS:

Mojo Jojo kidnaps the professor to lure the Powerpuff Girls to his lair and steal their powers. We also learn that Mojo has a previous connection to the professor that the girls were not aware of.

DISCUSSION QUESTIONS:

▸ Who do you think is most responsible for you becoming who you are?

▸ Have you ever had to deal with a new family member that you weren't sure you wanted around? Have you ever felt like others didn't want you around?

▸ If you are the youngest child, do you find it hard to be the "baby" of the family?

▸ Have you ever felt forgotten?

▸ Have you ever known someone who tries to act like someone else in order to be accepted by a group? Have you ever done that? What happened?

▸ Does God make us who we are? Are our "faults" God's fault? Explain.

CLOSING PRAYER:

God, you have made us what we are. What we do with the gifts you have given is up to us. What we choose to be is our own doing. Forgive us when we blame our problems on others. Help us know you are there to help shape and mold us into the servants you want us to become. Amen.

TOON TRIVIA

In perhaps a nod to the *Star Wars* movies, this episode reveals that the girls' greatest villain is, in fact, their father.

 OPTIONAL EXTRA

Have all the members of your group take their own names and scramble the letters to make new names. Make up name tags to use for the rest of the meeting.

45

SERIES
POWERPUFF GIRLS

EPISODE
POWERPUFF BLUFF

VOLUME TITLE:
**BUBBLEVICIOUS (VHS);
POWERPUFF BLUFF (DVD)**

THEMES: Acceptance, Behavior, Fitting In

SCRIPTURES:

- John 1:3: Everybody is welcome at Christ's table. EVERYbody!
- 1 Corinthians 8:6: God is the reason for everything.
- Colossians 1:16: All things are possible, if God says so.

SYNOPSIS:

Three dastardly crooks dress themselves as the Powerpuff Girls to escape prison. After escaping, they commit a series of crimes while dressed as our heroes. Only Ms. Bellum sees through the disguise and tells the mayor, who promptly (and mistakenly) throws the real Powerpuff Girls in jail.

DISCUSSION QUESTIONS:

- The Mayor loses his priceless porcelain poodle. What is your most prized possession? What would you do if someone broke it?
- Which is more precious to you—your most prized possession or your best friend?
- Why is it so important to fit in? Have you ever seen people completely change the way they look in order to be part of the crowd? What happened?
- Have you ever tried to change who you are in order to fit in? Talk about when something like this happened to you.
- When you were a young kid, whom did you want to be like? Whom do you admire now?

- Have you ever seen entire groups of people change based on whatever is popular? Give an example.
- Is it possible to take politeness too far? Give an example.
- Do we expect certain behaviors from girls that we don't expect from boys and vice versa?
- Who sets the standards of what is considered "proper behavior" for both genders?
- Have you ever been judged unfairly because of how you look? the people you hang out with? the way you worship?
- Read the Scripture verses cited above. What does the Bible say about "fitting in?"
- What do you think a cartoon Jesus might have said to the Powerpuff Girls in this episode?

Toon Trivia

One of the show's running gags, played nicely here, is that Ms. Bellum's face is never seen.

Closing Prayer:

Creator God, help us be who we are. We know that you have made us, and we know that you don't make mistakes. There is nothing wrong with us. We are your highest creation. Show us who you have made us to be, so that we can better serve you and love you. Amen.

OPTIONAL EXTRA

Have a tongue-twister contest. See which of your students can say, "Pirates from Providence have possibly purloined my priceless porcelain poodle" five times fast. Check your local dollar store for a porcelain dog as a prize.

46

SERIES
POWERPUFF GIRLS

EPISODE
UH OH DYNAMO

VOLUME TITLE:
**BUBBLEVICIOUS (VHS);
POWERPUFF BLUFF (DVD)**

THEMES: Growing Up, Parents

SCRIPTURES:

- Psalm 19: Everything God makes is good.
- Proverbs 11:14: Get good advice.
- Hebrews 5:14: You don't get to grow up all at once. Take your time.

SYNOPSIS:

While out for a day of fun, the professor and the girls are attacked by a giant fish balloon monster. The professor can't bear to watch his girls in danger, so he builds a giant robot to protect the girls and save the day.

DISCUSSION QUESTIONS:

- ▶ What does "letting go" mean for parents? What does it mean for you? Why do you think parents find it hard to let go? Why is it hard for you?
- ▶ Do your parents ever seem to be trying to keep you a child rather than allowing you to grow up? Explain.
- ▶ How are parents depicted in this episode?
- ▶ Do you think the parent in this episode is the monster's mother, or its father? What makes you think so?
- ▶ How does the monster's parent treat it?
- ▶ When the girls are in the giant robot, they find the professor has installed a "safety switch." What "safety switches" have your parents installed?

- ▸ Is it possible for the "protections" our parents put in place to do more harm than good? Explain.

- ▸ Can you think of a time when you really wanted your parents to bail you out, but that wasn't possible?

CLOSING PRAYER:

God, we are ready. We feel like we are on the launching pad, just waiting for the signal to blast off into our own lives. Help us make sure all systems are go, Lord. Make us ready, then clear the path. Amen.

TOON TRIVIA

This episode includes many references to classic giant robot shows like *Ultraman*, as well as modern ones such as *Power Rangers*.

 OPTIONAL EXTRA

Grab a few Japanese monster flicks from the video store. Show your group one or more of the typical scenes showing people running from the giant monster. Point out the way the cartoon pokes fun at this stereotypical image.

SERIES
ROGER RABBIT

EPISODE
TRAIL MIX-UP

VOLUME TITLE:
THE BEST OF ROGER RABBIT

47

THEMES: Co-dependency, Perseverance, Responsibility

SCRIPTURES:

- 1 Corinthians 9:24-27: Persistence pays off in the long run.
- Galatians 6:7-10: You get what you plant—so don't put off the planting season.
- Colossians 4:2: Pay attention!

SYNOPSIS:

Roger and Baby Herman go camping. Baby Herman gets away. Roger gets in trouble. Jessica Rabbit…uh…well, you'll see.

DISCUSSION QUESTIONS:

▸ When was the last time you pulled a friend's bacon out of the fire? When was the last time your bacon was rescued?

▸ Do you have a friend who just seems to get in trouble over and over? (No names, please.)

▸ Is there some point when we need to let our friends go ahead and get hurt?

▸ If you saw a kid sticking a bobby pin in the electrical outlet, would you stop him or her? If the kid kept doing it, would you let him or her get a shock and figure it out the hard way?

▸ Have you ever let a friend borrow your homework answers?

▸ Have you ever let a friend cheat off your test?

▸ Do you think some people take advantage of their friendships and behave however they want to without taking any personal responsibility?

▶ What would cause you to end a friendship? How many times do you need to get burned before you quit sticking your hand in the fire?

▶ What is tough love?

▶ What is co-dependency?

▶ What does the Bible tell us?

▶ Where would Jesus be in this cartoon?

CLOSING PRAYER:

God, we get ourselves in all sorts of trouble. That's bad enough, but sometimes we drag our friends along too.

Help us know when to back off. Help us bring our friends back from the edge before the saw gets them. Help us learn our lesson and let it stay learned. Amen.

TOON TRIVIA

Freeze-Frame Fun: Take a look at the bees. Also check out the reflection in Roger's eyes as he heads for Mt. Rushmore. If you have an early version of this tape, be sure to stop/pause on a poster in the lumber mill. Disney went to great lengths to recall the tapes and laser discs after the poster was discovered.

 OPTIONAL EXTRA

Serve trail mix—what else?

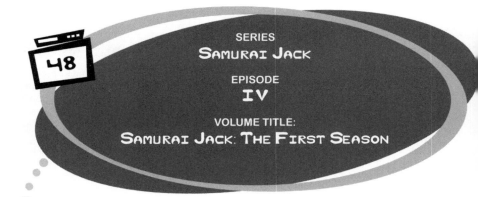

48

SERIES
SAMURAI JACK

EPISODE
IV

VOLUME TITLE:
SAMURAI JACK: THE FIRST SEASON

THEMES: Appearance, Judgment, Justice, Racism, Stereotypes

SCRIPTURES:

■ 1 Samuel 16:7: Looks aren't everything.

■ Luke 18:16: We must learn to be like children.

■ Ephesians 6:11-14: God will help you handle the hard stuff. Just let him.

SYNOPSIS:

Jack helps a small blue creature re-capture his rampaging woolly. The blue guys invite Jack to stay for a party. Jack wanders off alone and finds the woollies penned and mistreated. Jack realizes he may have made a mistake and frees the woollies from captivity.

DISCUSSION QUESTIONS:

▶ Have you ever misjudged someone?

▶ Have you ever been judged on the basis of your appearance?

▶ At what point does "judging" become racism?

▶ How could Jack have done things differently?

▶ Once we have developed an opinion of some person or some group, why is it so hard to let go of that opinion? Is it their job to prove that we have misjudged them?

▶ Can we liken this situation to the way African Americans have been treated throughout our history—and today?

- Jokes about certain ethnic groups (i.e. Polish jokes) are no longer politically acceptable, although they once were not considered offensive. Are there any groups today that it seems perfectly normal to make fun of?

- What kinds of generalizations are made about teenagers in today's culture? Are any of them true? Do you find any of them offensive?

- Draw some analogies between Jack's story and your own life. How do your parents keep you in line? How do you react when the chains get too tight? Who is the "Jack" in your life that can help you get some dignity back?

- How does the Bible empower you, even if it seems like you have no power at the moment?

- What are you going to do when the cage is open?

TOON TRIVIA

This is one of the few episodes where we see Jack with his hair down.

CLOSING PRAYER:

God of all, as we are growing up, sometimes it feels like we are in a cage. Help us be patient. Help us understand that our parents are not jailers. Help us wait until the time is right for our freedom. Amen.

 OPTIONAL EXTRA

Critchellite Tag: Put two students in a ten-foot circle in your church's fellowship hall or parking lot. Give each kid a cardboard tube. (You can paint or decorate these to look like the "cattle prods" in the episode if you wish.) Say "go." The Critchellite who tags his opponent the most times in 30 seconds wins.

SERIES
SAMURAI JACK

EPISODE
VII

VOLUME TITLE:
SAMURAI JACK: THE FIRST SEASON

THEMES: Consequences, Disabilities, Faith

SCRIPTURES:

- Jeremiah 17:10: God knows what you really need.
- Matthew 6:33: Shortcuts will often lead you into a brick wall.
- Luke 12:15: Better clothes won't make you a better person.

SYNOPSIS:

Jack hears about a magic wishing well guarded by three great warriors. He watches as an entire army attempts to take the well and is driven back by the three archers. Jack determines the archers are blind and blindfolds himself, relying on his other senses and his training (much like how Luke Skywalker learned how to use the force in the original *Star Wars*). In the end Jack destroys the well, after realizing that the granting of wishes always comes with a catch.

DISCUSSION QUESTIONS:

- Why did Jack destroy the well? Would you have done so?
- Have you ever heard the phrase, "There's no such thing as a free lunch?" What does it mean?
- Have you ever wished you could take a magic pill so you could ace a test? play an instrument? score a goal? Are such things possible?
- Do we appreciate something more when we work for it?

- Old Joke: A visitor to New York City asks a local man, "How do I get to Carnegie Hall?" The second man says, "Practice." What's the lesson beyond the humor?

- How does it feel to be "this close" to a goal only to have it disappear?

- Does the "easy road" usually come with a price tag? Explain.

- How is our faith journey like Jack's journey home?

- How did Jack defeat the archers?

- List three of your own goals. (Note: If your goal is something you can accomplish tomorrow by being the person you are right now, it's too small!) What steps are you taking today to try to achieve those goals?

- Jack opened his other senses in order to defeat the archers. What parts of yourself need to be open in order to achieve your goals?

CLOSING PRAYER:

Invite the youth to pray in silence with you: "Dear God, show us what we need to do to become the person you want us to be." (Pause.) Amen.

 OPTIONAL EXTRA

See if your group can use their other senses as Jack does. Create a "sword" out of rolled up newspaper or a large cardboard tube. Blindfold one person and then allow the rest of your group to throw balls of wadded-up newspaper at the blindfolded person. (Note: It's interesting to watch the body language of kids who are listening so hard you can almost hear them listen.)

THEMES: Betrayal, Honesty, Integrity, Love

SCRIPTURES:

- Psalm 27: Celebrate being alive.
- Isaiah 33:15-16: Live right. Get cookies.
- 1 John 4:7-12: Love = God. It's not hard math.

SYNOPSIS:

Jack finds an underwater city. He has heard that the merfolk of this city possess a time machine. They agree to let Jack use the time machine, but then betray him to Aku for their own purposes. Aku then betrays the merfolk, who must ask Jack to rescue them. In the end all Jack asks for is some fish.

DISCUSSION QUESTIONS:

- Have you ever trusted someone who turned out to be "selling you to Aku"?
- Have you ever sold out a friend? Explain.
- Jack helps the people who tried to trade him to Aku. Could you have done this?
- How does this compare with Jesus' life and death?
- How can you show love to someone who hurts you? Is there ever a point where we should just walk away?
- Why do you think Jack did not ask to use the time machine at the end of the episode? Could you have just walked away?

- ▶ What is integrity?

- ▶ How many times do you have to forgive someone? Should there be a limit on forgiveness?

- ▶ Why is forgiveness so hard sometimes?

- ▶ What does it mean when we pray, "Forgive us our trespasses, as we forgive those who trespass against us"? How does that theme apply here?

CLOSING PRAYER:

God, not everyone has our best interests in mind. Help us see when we are making bad decisions. Help us forgive those who try to harm us. Let us be forgiven for the times when we hurt others. Amen.

TOON TRIVIA

One of the voice actors in this episode seems to be doing an impression of Alec Guinness. (Guinness played Obi-Wan Kenobi in the first *Star Wars* movies.) The actor doing the voice in this cartoon is Mark Hamill, who played Luke Skywalker in the *Star Wars* films.

 OPTIONAL EXTRA

Have a merfolk race. Wrap each kid's legs inside a garbage bag (tail) and have the kids crawl like fish out of water to a finish line. Serve goldfish crackers with this movie.

51

THEMES: Conflict, Cooperation, Forgiveness, Stubbornness

SCRIPTURES:

■ Psalm 106: God settles things.

■ Proverbs 16:17-22: Listen. Don't talk.

■ Romans 12:4-5: We must learn to work together.

SYNOPSIS:

Jack meets a Scotsman halfway across a bridge. Neither is willing to give the other the right of way. Aku's hired hit men bind Jack and the Scotsman together. Eventually, they must work together to free themselves and defeat Aku's henchmen.

DISCUSSION QUESTIONS:

▸ Would you have given the right of way to the other person on the bridge? Explain.

▸ What would have happened if Jack (or the Scotsman) had simply moved out of the way?

▸ Have you ever been in a situation where it seems God has "handcuffed" you to your biggest problem? How did it go?

▸ How does this story compare to the parable of the prodigal son?

▸ What happens when you disagree with someone and focus on winning the argument rather than finding a solution?

- How does this episode end? How can you make your arguments end that way? (No, not by drinking, but by becoming friends.)
- Thinking Deeper: What if Jack and the Scotsman represent two sides of us?

TOON TRIVIA

Episode XI is the first episode in which Jack smiles.

CLOSING PRAYER:

Peacemaking God, bring us together. We have so many ways to separate ourselves from each other. Unite us this day. Show us that we can learn from each other. Help us work together. Amen.

 OPTIONAL EXTRA

The Scotsman appears to be caber-tossing, a Scottish game in which participants heave a log in the air and have it flip once before landing. Try playing this game with your youth. Make a caber out of a two-by-four, or see if you can get your hands on one of the big tubes that carpet comes wrapped on.

SERIES
SAMURAI JACK

EPISODE
XVIII

VOLUME TITLE:
SAMURAI JACK: THE FIRST SEASON

THEMES: Facing Problems, Faith, Family, Strength

SCRIPTURES:

- Psalm 73: Listen to God, not stupid people.
- Isaiah 40:29-31: When you think you can't go on, God will give you a boost.
- Philippians 4:13: You are God's. God does not make mistakes.

SYNOPSIS:

Jack travels from village to village and sees the death and destruction wrought by a team of killer robots created by a man named Extor. Extor apparently built the robots for Aku, but then was betrayed by him. Jack battles the robots with a bionic arm built by Extor. Jack must defeat the final robot on his own by calling on the spirits of his ancestors for help.

DISCUSSION QUESTIONS:

- What is the greatest challenge you've ever faced?
- Have you ever gone up against impossible odds with the full support of friends and family and lost anyway? Have you ever won?
- Where does your strength come from?
- Name some people from the Scriptures who went up against the impossible and won.
- Who is your Extor—the one you can go to for advice and help? The most knowledgeable?

- Who is your greatest enemy? (No names out loud, please.) What power does that person have over you? What did Jesus tell us to do about those who would harm us? What did David say in the Psalms?

- Who is your "only hope"? Who do you call on when every other possibility has been exhausted?

- Why do we often call on God only as a last resort? Why do we sometimes pray only after we've expended all our efforts and finally hit rock-bottom? Why do we wait?

- Think about Jack's robot arm. What "modifications" have you made when facing something that seemed unbeatable?

- In the end Jack calls on the strength of his family to help him defeat the enemy. Do you find it easy to call on your family for help? Why, or why not?

CLOSING PRAYER:

Strong and knowing God, help us find the strength to keep going when it feels like we can't go anymore. Help us learn to call on you. Help us trust our families. Help make us strong when others need our help. Amen.

OPTIONAL EXTRA

Give your students 15 or 20 minutes to create Samurai Swords out of newspaper and then have battles. Create a 10' x 10' square on the floor out of masking tape. Divide the square in half. Score one point for each "hit" (below the neck). First player to seven points wins.

53

SERIES
SAMURAI JACK

EPISODE
XIX

VOLUME TITLE:
SAMURAI JACK: THE FIRST SEASON

THEMES: Bullies, Faith, The Past, Strength

SCRIPTURES:

- Deuteronomy 9:2-3: God has cleared the path so you can do what you have to do.
- Psalm 82: God will deal with those who need dealing with.
- Proverbs 19:21: If God says so, it will happen. Have a little faith.

SYNOPSIS:

While traveling, Jack finds himself in his boyhood town. (Of course, he must fight and defeat some evil feline robots on the way.) While wandering, Jack begins to remember significant moments in his life and how those events led him to become who he is now.

DISCUSSION QUESTIONS:

- Have you ever gone back to a place you haven't been in a long time? Did it seem different from what you remembered? In what way?
- Have you ever gotten together with a former best friend whom you'd lost touch with? What happened?
- What has been the biggest change about you in the last five years?
- What is your favorite childhood memory?
- Like the man on the bridge, we all face challenges that stand between where we are today and our destinies. What stands between you and your destiny?

- What makes a person "mighty"?

- Where does inner strength come from?

- How do you know if something is "meant to be"? Give an example.

- Have you ever had to deal with people who just seem to take pleasure in making your life difficult? What happens when you fight them on their own terms?

- Read the Scriptures cited above. What does the Bible say about facing your enemies? facing your destiny?

- What is an "obstacle" you are facing right now? If you are comfortable, share it with the group, and see if you can come up with a creative solution together.

TOON TRIVIA

The scene where "young Jack" sees a man deal with three villains on the bridge is a nice little nod to a famous series of Japanese cartoons and books called *Lone Wolf and Cub*.

CLOSING PRAYER:

Mighty and everlasting God, we don't get to know what you know. You watch from your place, and sometimes we disappoint you. Help us not to do that. Give us just a small hint of what is to come, and we will be your servants forever. Amen.

 OPTIONAL EXTRA

Ask your students to bring in their school pictures from first or second grade. Have each student make a list of ten things that he or she would tell the kid in the picture if it were possible to travel back in time and meet yourself.

54

SERIES
THE SIMPSONS

EPISODE
BART GETS AN F

VOLUME TITLE:
THE COMPLETE SECOND SEASON

THEMES: Integrity, Prayer, Siblings

SCRIPTURES:

- Job 22:23-29: Don't let the world get you down.
- Psalm 3: God, save us from prisons of our own creation.
- Matthew 6:5-6: It's a prayer, not a Broadway production.

SYNOPSIS:

After a series of gigantic missteps, Bart is on the verge of failing the fourth grade. With just one chance left, he falls to his knees in desperation and prays for a miracle. He gets one. Of course, what he does with it is another matter…

DISCUSSION QUESTIONS:

▸ What do you think Bart will be doing when he's thirty?

▸ Do you agree with Lisa that prayer is "the last refuge of a scoundrel"?

▸ When do you pray most often? Do you pray before you take a test?

▸ Have you ever had to deal with a sibling who seemed to do everything better than you?

▸ People often behave in ways that match other people's expectations for them. People expect Bart to mess around and get low grades, and he usually does. Is Bart a product of his environment? Would he do better in school if his teachers expected him to be a better student?

▸ Do you feel sorry for Bart? Explain.

▸ What is so striking about Bart's prayer? Why was the answer ironic?

- Do you think God's answers to our prayers come with strings attached?

- Does God have a sense of humor?

- Have you ever prayed for something and gotten it? How did you react?

- Have you ever prayed for something that didn't happen? Explain.

- Have you ever not gotten something you prayed for and then realized later that you were probably better off without it? Talk about that.

- If Bart had not asked his teacher to grade the test immediately, he never would have "demonstrated applied learning" and would have failed. Is this grace? Did Bart get grace from the teacher or from God?

TOON TRIVIA

Did anyone else see the school nurse picking up tongue depressors and putting them back in the jar?

CLOSING PRAYER:

Loving God, we are praying to you now. We're not asking for snow or test answers, but just to know you a little better. Speak to us, God. We are listening. Amen.

 OPTIONAL EXTRA

Try the ten-second wrong answer quiz. Prepare a list of easy questions (What color is the sky? How many fingers do you have?). Have your group break into teams. Have players come forward one at a time, and ask each person five questions in ten seconds. To get a point, the person must give the wrong answer to each question. (It's harder than it sounds.)

SERIES
THE SIMPSONS

EPISODE
BART THE GENIUS

VOLUME TITLE:
THE COMPLETE FIRST SEASON

55

THEMES: Acceptance, Grades, School

SCRIPTURES:

- Exodus 31:2-11: God gives gifts that are just for you.
- 1 Samuel 16:7: How God sees us is different from how the world sees us.
- Romans 12:2: If everybody else jumped off a bridge…

SYNOPSIS:

Bart switches tests with a smart kid and winds up in a school for gifted students. Despite feeling that he doesn't belong, Bart sticks with the program because of the newfound attention he is getting from his family (particularly his dad). In the end Bart must "come clean" (pun intended), and he confesses his shame to Homer.

DISCUSSION QUESTIONS:

▷ Do we put too much emphasis on grades?

▷ Listen to the way Mrs. Krabapple talks about the test. Do you ever feel like schools really operate this way? Can you think of a better way to show how students learn?

▷ Did you notice that even in the gifted school, there are still students who will laugh at others and put them down for being different? What does that tell you?

▷ Would you rather be the star quarterback, the coach, or the team owner?

- Some students are "gifted" in the way they learn. What are some other gifts? What are your gifts? Read Ephesians 4:7-13. What are the gifts that God sends? Do you have any of these?

- Have you ever felt like you walked into the wrong class and had to stay for the lecture? Talk about it.

- The Simpsons go to the opera because they think that's what they are supposed to do, but Homer and the kids have more fun making flatulent noises. Would you rather go to an opera or a farting contest? Explain.

- Is Bart's lying a sin if it results in a closer relationship with his father? Do you believe Bart's speech at the end of the episode?

- Read Romans 8:28. How does this apply to Bart's life?

CLOSING PRAYER:

God, you know who we really are. You know us when we lie for what we think are the right reasons. You know us when we turn ourselves green—and you love us anyway. Thank you, God. Sometimes we need all the help we can get. Amen.

 OPTIONAL EXTRA

The MENSA test is available at *http://www.mensa.org/index.html*. Borrow some questions and see if you have any geniuses in your group. Then go outside and mix some vinegar and baking soda for fun.

SERIES
THE SIMPSONS

EPISODE
HOMER'S NIGHT OUT

VOLUME TITLE:
THE COMPLETE FIRST SEASON

56

THEMES: Forgiveness, Role Models

SCRIPTURES:

- Numbers 11:17: Life is group work.
- Matthew 18:22: Forgive as you want to be forgiven.
- James 2:13: You get what you give.

SYNOPSIS:

After weeks of waiting, Bart finally gets his spy camera. He takes a picture of his own father with an exotic dancer that is soon all over Springfield. Marge is mad at Homer and tells him the only way he can earn her forgiveness is if he will take Bart to see the dancer, so Bart can see that she is a real person, not an object.

DISCUSSION QUESTIONS:

▸ Have you ever ordered something through the mail and found when it arrived that it wasn't quite what you were after?

▸ Has anyone ever taken your picture or recorded a conversation without your permission? Explain.

▸ What did Homer do wrong?

▸ Was Bart wrong to take the photo?

▸ Was Marge overreacting?

▸ What did you think of Marge's requirement for her forgiveness?

▸ Should forgiveness come with conditions? Is God's forgiveness conditional?

- What is the longest amount of time you've ever stayed mad at someone? What is the longest anyone has ever stayed mad at you?

- Have you ever apologized without knowing what you were apologizing for? Have you ever apologized without meaning it?

- Do you think Homer's statement, "I'd rather feel my wife's soft breath on the back of my neck..." was a compliment?

- How do you ask for forgiveness? Is there anyone who has asked for your forgiveness and you haven't given it yet?

- What is your reaction to the phrase, "Forgive and forget"? Can you forgive without forgetting? Should you?

- Read the Scriptures cited above. What does the Bible say about forgiveness? Who is being the most "biblical" in this episode?

CLOSING PRAYER:

God, sometimes we do things that seem unforgivable. Sometimes our actions hurt other people; sometimes they hurt you. We are grateful that you don't keep a list of our wrongs, because we know it would be a long list. Help us forgive others as you forgive us. Amen.

OPTIONAL EXTRA

Take a series of photos of items in your church from bizarre angles. Make photocopies of these pictures or hang them up and see if your group can find the spots where you took the photos.

57

SERIES
THE SIMPSONS

EPISODE
HOMER'S ODYSSEY

VOLUME TITLE:
THE COMPLETE FIRST SEASON

THEMES: Integrity, Justice

SCRIPTURES:

- Leviticus 19:11: Life rules.
- Job 2:9-10: Everything (good and bad) comes from God. It's all a gift.
- Proverbs 10 (the whole chapter): You want to be happy? This is "Plan A."

SYNOPSIS:

When Homer gets fired from the nuclear power plant, he becomes a consumer crusader. Later, Homer is offered a new job and a raise from Mr. Burns if he will compromise his principles. Homer can't bring himself to lie to those who have come to respect him.

DISCUSSION QUESTIONS:

- What is integrity? *(A good working definition: Integrity is the kind of person you are when no one is looking.)*
- If the cashier at the drive-through gave you too much change, would you keep it?
- Would you report someone at your job who was stealing change from the cash drawer? What if it were $20? What if they were embezzling large amounts of money?
- Have you ever cheated at a game? Have you ever caught someone cheating? (No names, please.) Talk about it.
- When is it hardest to be a person of integrity? Who do you know who has the most integrity? Can you name a person in the news recently who has

a great deal of integrity? How about someone who lacks integrity?

▸ There are a lot of Bible verses about integrity. Read a few of the suggested verses. How do they relate to Homer? How do they relate to your own life?

CLOSING PRAYER:

God, help us be the same people you want us to be even when no one is looking. Cutting corners won't get us ahead in your eyes. Let us be the servants we are called to be. Amen.

TOON TRIVIA

The complete lyrics to "John Henry: The Steel Driving Man" can be found at *http://www.ibib-lio.org/john_henry/index.html*

OPTIONAL EXTRA

Hold an "integrity test" at a local mall or supermarket. Tack a five dollar bill to a community bulletin board with a note that says, "Bill, here's the five bucks I owe you." Have your group stand at a distance and see how long it takes for the bill to disappear. (Note: You might have to take three or four bills with you to make your point.)

SERIES
THE SIMPSONS

EPISODE
HOMER THE HERETIC

VOLUME TITLE:
THE COMPLETE THIRD SEASON

THEMES: Church Attendance, Faith, Grace

SCRIPTURES:

- Psalm 89: God takes care of his own.
- Romans 4:4-5: Too big to lift? Ask God. He's pretty strong.
- 2 Corinthians 5:16-21: Look inside a person. Give 'em another chance.

SYNOPSIS:

Homer decides not to go to church. Rather than being damned, he has a wonderful day. Marge prays. Homer has a vision and starts his own religion. Later, Homer is saved from a burning house by the happy Christian Ned Flanders. Homer eventually gets to have a heart-to-heart with the Big Guy himself.

DISCUSSION QUESTIONS:

- Did you find this episode offensive in any way?
- What is a heretic? *The word comes from "heresy" which originally meant "choice," but now normally refers to a belief or opinion that contradicts the norm, especially orthodox religious perspectives.*
- Is there anything wrong with calling Homer a heretic? Explain.
- Is Kurt Cobain in heaven? Will Eminem or Marilyn Manson get in? How about Adolf Hitler or Osama bin Laden? Who gets to make that decision?
- At what point does witnessing to your neighbor just become annoying?
- Did God punish Homer for not going to church? Do you think you'll get punished if you don't go to church (not by your parents, but by God)?

- There are so many different religions—who decides which one is right? The "snake-handlers" worship the same God that other Christians do. Why are our ways of worshipping so different?

- Why do we judge others by how they believe?

- Is there any religion that you consider just plain wrong?

- Do you know your denomination's history? How has it evolved?

- Do you think going to church is an essential part of being a Christian? The Bible has a lot of references to gathering for worship and building the church. Is it possible to do any of those things from your couch?

- What is your favorite part of worship? What was the best worship experience you ever had?

- Notice that Homer is not an atheist or agnostic—he does not question God's existence, only his own religion. Have you ever felt like that? Explain. Did you feel like you were wrong for feeling that way? Explain.

- Where did Homer experience grace in this episode? Other than in the dream, how did God make himself known to Homer? How does God make himself known to us?

TOON TRIVIA

Notice that God has five fingers. Everyone else has the standard cartoon four.

CLOSING PRAYER:

God, bring us closer to you. Find a way. Get our attention. Reach in through the distractions we create and put your face in ours. Strengthen our faith so that we know you are with us always, even when we don't see you. Amen.

 OPTIONAL EXTRA

Serve toaster waffles with caramel ice-cream topping as a snack.

SERIES
THE SIMPSONS

EPISODE
KRUSTY GETS BUSTED

VOLUME TITLE:
THE COMPLETE FIRST SEASON

THEMES: Honesty, Integrity, Justice, Role Models

SCRIPTURES:

- Psalm 25: With God's help I can do anything.
- Daniel 3:1-30: Can you love God even if it's going to hurt?
- 1 Thessalonians 2:13: Listen for God, and God will make himself known.

SYNOPSIS:

Bart's hero, Krusty the Klown, is framed for robbing the Quick-E Mart. Homer is the only witness and must identify his son's hero in court. Bart and Lisa discover that Krusty has been framed by his sidekick, Sideshow Bob, and set out to free Krusty.

DISCUSSION QUESTIONS:

▷ Who was your hero when you were Bart's age? Who is your hero now?

▷ What if you found out that your hero had a deep dark secret? Does everybody have such a secret?

▷ How valuable is honesty in today's culture?

▷ Would you lie to help a friend avoid a detention? grounding? a traffic ticket? a prison sentence?

▷ What lengths would you go to protect your child from harm? How far would your parents go to protect you?

▷ What is a "hard lesson"?

- Have you ever heard your parents say, "You'll understand one day"? Do you think that's true? What things are you still waiting to understand?

- Sideshow Bob begins reading the classics and singing Cole Porter and the kids respond. What was your favorite show when you were a kid? Have you watched it recently? Do you think kids' television is more sophisticated than it used to be?

- What gimmicky toys do you own?

- Have you ever been betrayed by a best friend?

- How important is it to stand up and speak the truth, even if it hurts? What happened to Moses? *(He had to run off and live as a shepherd.)* What happened to Peter and Paul? *(They got arrested.)* We know what happened to Jesus.

- What did you think of Reverend Lovejoy's attitude?

- Have you ever jumped on the bandwagon?

- What is the most honest thing you've ever done?

- Have you ever lost faith in someone? (No names, please.) Did you get it back?

- Homer thought he knew what had happened, but he was incorrect. Was he wrong to testify?

TOON TRIVIA

Sideshow Bob refers to Lisa and Bart as "you meddling kids," a phrase used by the "bad guys" in nearly every episode of the original *Scooby Doo* television series.

CLOSING PRAYER:

God of laughter and children, let us stand up for what is right. Help us not to hide behind the potato chips when things are going bad. Help us feel your ever-present hand on our shoulder, especially when we are forced to make the hard decisions. Amen.

 OPTIONAL EXTRA

Serve microwavable burritos as a snack.

SERIES
THE SIMPSONS

EPISODE
LIKE FATHER LIKE CLOWN

VOLUME TITLE:
THE COMPLETE FIRST SEASON

60

THEMES: Calling, Career, Parents

SCRIPTURES:

- Psalm 69: I'm in over my head here, God. Help!
- Proverbs 4:3: Advice from Dad.
- 1 Corinthians 12:4-7: Everybody gets gifts. Use them.

SYNOPSIS:

Krusty visits the Simpsons' home, and the family discovers that he is Jewish. Bart and Lisa attempt to reunite him with his father.

DISCUSSION QUESTIONS:

▷ If you asked them, what would your parents say they want you to do when you get out of college?

▷ Barring any excuses about college or money or anything else, what would you love to do for a living when you grow up?

▷ Is there a difference between what you want to be and what you want to do for a living? Do we usually make that distinction?

▷ Why was the Rabbi disappointed?

▷ How serious are you about your religion? (Not your faith, but your religion.)

▷ How much does your family respect tradition? Would you be kicked out of the house if you disappointed your parents? Is there any career choice (other than youth ministry) that would disappoint your parents?

- What is a calling? Do you think God would call someone to be a clown? a cop? a minister? a fast food worker?

- If you had a very real dream one night in which God appeared to you and said, "I want you to become a minister," do you think you could? How about a youth minister? What if God told you to become a missionary in Africa?

- Krusty says, "Dad, I want to make people laugh." His father says, "Life is not fun. Life is serious." What do you think?

- Read the Psalm. See if you can re-write it with the title "Psalm of Krusty."

- What would Krusty say to Jesus if Jesus were a guest on the show?

- We know that the Bible says to honor your father and mother. What does the Bible tell parents to do?

- What Bible story would you like to see in a pop-up book?

CLOSING PRAYER:

Laughing God, you are the author of joy. Rain down laughter and giggles on us. Show us that life is good, and that we are players on your stage. Keep us joyful. Amen.

 OPTIONAL EXTRA

You can purchase clown noses from US Toy Company *(www.ustoy.com)* for less than a buck apiece. Pass these out to your kids and play some classic party games like pin the tail on the donkey or musical chairs.

61

SERIES
THE SIMPSONS

EPISODE
MOANING LISA

VOLUME TITLE:
THE COMPLETE FIRST SEASON

THEMES: Friendship, Parents, Self-acceptance, Unhappiness

SCRIPTURES:

■ Psalm 16: God will build me a hurricane shelter.

■ Proverbs 15:13: It's all in the attitude.

■ Ephesians 4:7-12: God has a gift for you. Are you ready?

SYNOPSIS:

Lisa seeks to find meaning in life and the universe, but finds the sadness that only a second grader can find. She meets a kindred spirit in blues musician Bleeding Gums Murphy. Marge tries to help by reciting all of the happy lessons she learned as a child, only to realize that she isn't being completely honest with herself or her daughter.

DISCUSSION QUESTIONS:

▷ What's the saddest thing you can think of? Have you ever felt that sad?

▷ Is sadness a matter of perspective? Do movie stars get sad? If so, should they bother complaining about it?

▷ What lessons did Marge's mother teach her? What was wrong with what she was taught?

▷ What happens when you push a beach ball below the surface of the pool? What happens when we do the same with our emotions?

▷ Do you feel like you have to put on a "happy face" in order to be accepted? Does you church have room for people who are sad?

- What is a kindred spirit? What did Lisa find in Bleeding Gums Murphy? Who is your Bleeding Gums? If you don't have such a friend, how would you go about finding one?

- How do you best express yourself? Music? Art? Mathematical equations?

- How are you being raised differently from the way your parents were raised? How will you raise your own children differently? Is there only one right way?

- Do you think your parents ever feel like they are messing up? How can we cut parents some slack? What do you think they need to feel like they are important?

- Pretend you are Lisa's Sunday school teacher. What would you tell her?

- How is Marge's advice to Lisa at the end of the episode like the Scripture readings?

TOON TRIVIA

Notice how much the video boxers look like Bart and Homer.

CLOSING PRAYER:

God, we are happy. We are sad. We are angry. We are tired. Sometimes we are all these things at the same time. Help us understand that it's okay to feel what we feel. Help us remember that no matter how lonely we may feel sometimes...we are never alone. Amen.

 OPTIONAL EXTRA

If you have a guitar player, sax player, and/or harmonica player in your group, let them brush up on their blues as you write a song together. (If no musicians are available, you can sing the Bleeding Gums sax part, and let your students fill in lyrics like Lisa.) You can write a blues song about being a youth minister.

62

SERIES
The Simpsons

EPISODE
Simpson and Delilah

VOLUME TITLE:
The Complete Second Season

THEMES: Appearance, Judgment, Stereotypes

SCRIPTURES:

- Matthew 7:1-6: It's called the boomerang effect.
- 2 Corinthians 5:16-21: A note from the God of second chances.
- Ephesians 2:11-22: You're a servant. Act like it.

SYNOPSIS:

Homer discovers a miraculous new treatment for baldness and reaps the rewards at work. But when his hair goes, so does his self-confidence. Homer hires a secretary named Carl who helps him find the confidence to be a leader.

DISCUSSION QUESTIONS:

This episode's title comes from the story of Samson and Delilah. Begin with a quick overview of that biblical story, which is found in Judges 16. Samson's power comes from his hair, which has never been cut. Delilah keeps trying to figure out the source of his power. After she seduces him, he finally tells her. She cuts Samson's hair off, chains him to a temple, and pokes out his eyes.

- Is there a stereotype that goes along with hair?
- Who's got the greatest hair in Hollywood? Name some famous bald people.
- Have you ever been judged by your appearance? your clothing? your accent? What was it like?
- Why do you suppose we make snap judgments about people?
- Why is the phrase "first impressions count" true? Should it be?

- Is Carl gay? How do you know? What judgments did you make? What stereotypes did you rely on to get that answer?

- Is beauty a gift? If we can call musical, artistic, or sports ability a gift, why is it hard to consider beauty a gift?

- Is it hard to feel sorry for a supermodel? Why, or why not?

- Who is more appearance-conscious—guys or girls?

- There's a cliché that goes, "Don't hate me because I'm beautiful." Is there any truth there? Do people get hated because they are good-looking?

- God puts aside the ways the world judges us and looks at the kind of people we are. Read 1 Samuel 16:7. How could we apply that to Homer?

TOON TRIVIA

This episode was one of the first times a man kissed another man on prime-time television. When censors complained, producers of *The Simpsons* used the "Elmer Fudd loophole," reminding them that Bugs Bunny had kissed Elmer numerous times. Censors let the kiss go.

CLOSING PRAYER:

Creator God, you have made us all in your image. All of us. Help us look beneath the surface and see the soul as you do. Help us not to judge people by their clothes or their appearance. Give us clean souls, so we can be seen for who we truly are. Amen.

OPTIONAL EXTRA

Serve fish sticks with copious amounts of tartar sauce as a snack. Take one of the suggested Scriptures and have the kids spell the words out fo-net-ick-lee.

63

SERIES
THE SIMPSONS

EPISODE
SIMPSONS ROASTING ON AN OPEN FIRE

VOLUME TITLE:
THE COMPLETE FIRST SEASON

THEMES: Christmas, The Holidays, Parents, Sacrifice

SCRIPTURES:

- Deuteronomy 11:18-21: This stuff is important. Listen.
- Psalm 50: God gets to be in charge.
- Proverbs 23:13-14: Nothing wrong with a swat on the bum.

SYNOPSIS:

Homer doesn't get his Christmas bonus. Bart gets a tattoo (then has it removed). In a last-ditch effort to make some Christmas money, Homer becomes a department store Santa. After taking his earnings to the track, Homer goes home with the best Christmas gift of all—"Something to share our love."

DISCUSSION QUESTIONS:

▸ What is the best Christmas gift you ever received? Now think in a non-material way—what is the best Christmas gift you ever received?

▸ Lisa's Christmas list consists of one item: a pony. Was there one thing you always wanted for Christmas but never got? What was it?

▸ When it comes to Christmas decorations, is your family more like the Flanders or the Simpsons? (Notice that this episode was before the Flanders family became the Christian comic relief.)

▸ Bart is proud of his dad for "lowering" himself to provide for his family. Is there anything your parents wouldn't do for you? Would they get a second job? post bail if you were arrested? show up and listen at every single one of your Christmas concerts?

- Does your family have any "Marge's sisters"? What did you think of the way they treated Homer?
- Do you think schools have gone overboard to be politically correct? How do you think you'd feel if you were Jewish or a Jehovah's Witness? Would it bother you if your school had a Christmas pageant? Should the separation of church and state be complete?
- Is there a Christmas miracle in this episode? Is it possible God wanted Homer to gamble so he could take the dog home to his family?
- How is Homer like Charlie Brown in "A Charlie Brown Christmas" (Lesson 23)?
- Unlike the Peanuts special, there's no Linus in this show to explain the true meaning of Christmas. What message do we get from the episode?

TOON TRIVIA

Watch carefully as Bart's friend turns from an African American to a red-headed white (yellow?) kid.

CLOSING PRAYER:

God, we don't get to choose our families, but we can choose to love and support one another. Help us remember that "sharing our love" with those around us is a gift you have given us. Remind us that the ability to love at all comes from you. Help us share our love with our families, friends, and our communities. Amen.

 OPTIONAL EXTRA

See how many different variations of classic Christmas carols your students already know. Then see if you can write your own carol about your senior pastor.

64

SERIES
THE SIMPSONS

EPISODE
THERE'S NO DISGRACE LIKE HOME

VOLUME TITLE:
THE COMPLETE FIRST SEASON

THEMES: Family, Getting Along, Relationships

SCRIPTURES:

- Psalm 27: It's all about God.
- 2 Corinthians 6:11-13: Open up a little and see what you can learn.
- Ephesians 6:1-4: Family is group work.

SYNOPSIS:

After an embarrassing experience at the company picnic, Homer tries to make his family "normal." The first step is spying on the neighbors. The second: family therapy. Finally, he gets a new television.

DISCUSSION QUESTIONS:

- What is a normal family?
- How normal is your family?
- How has "normal" changed since your parents were kids? Your grandparents?
- The happy family got to go to heaven. Homer had to get in the car from hell. Have you ever felt this way about your family?
- Have you ever seen a kid walk fifteen paces behind his parents at the mall? Have you ever done that? Why?
- Is it normal for parents to embarrass their children? Vice versa?
- Why do family members say things to one another that they would never say to friends?

- Can family problems be fixed? Is there any such thing as familial bliss?

- When someone turns on the television at the company picnic, the children all stop playing and become zombies. What would happen if you made a pact with your family to turn off the TV for a week? (Other than *The Simpsons*, of course.)

- How does God want us to treat our families? Do you think some families are just proof that God has a sense of humor?

- Families change just as individuals change. Your parents are not the same people they were when you were four years old. How have your parents grown since you were a young child? How have they grown since you became a teenager?

- Read Luke 2:41-52. What would you do if you stayed behind when your family went on a trip? What is Mary's response? Do you think she and Joseph were angry? Is Jesus giving his parents an attitude here?

- If you could change one thing about your family, what would it be?

- Read Galatians 5:13-14. How can you apply these verses to your family relationships?

TOON TRIVIA

The line "One of us, one of us" at the company picnic could be a reference to a creepy 1932 horror cult film called *Freaks*.

CLOSING PRAYER:

God, you gave me this family. Now help me deal with it. Each day is something new. Each day is a new opportunity. Help us be functional. Teach us how to love, work together, and help one another grow. Amen.

 OPTIONAL EXTRA

Serve Jell-O. Lots and lots of Jell-O. Jell-O with marshmallows. Jell-O with shaved carrots. All colors, shapes, and sizes. Just use lots!

65

SERIES
SpongeBob SquarePants

EPISODE
Big Pink Loser

VOLUME TITLE:
Tide & Seek

THEMES: Peer pressure, Role Models, Self-esteem

SCRIPTURES:

- Deuteronomy 6:7-9: This is important—Be yourself!
- Romans 12:1-2: Make every day count.
- Romans 13:9: It's called common courtesy.

SYNOPSIS:

Patrick wishes he were special. So he changes his personality to match that of the person he admires the most—SpongeBob.

DISCUSSION QUESTIONS:

▷ Why do we like our achievements to be recognized? Is it necessary? Is it part of human nature?

▷ What was the greatest recognition you have received? (It can be an award, a grade, your name in the paper, or just a comment from someone.)

▷ What makes you different from anyone else?

▷ Do you know kids in your school who completely change themselves to fit in? Have you ever tried to change to fit in?

▷ Have you ever bought a particular shirt or CD because "everybody else" had it?

▷ Why is it so hard for some people to like themselves the way they are?

▷ Why is it so hard for some people to accept others the way they are?

- Does every school have a "cool kids" lunch table? What table do you sit at? Have you ever wanted to switch tables? How did that go?

- If the coolest, most popular kid in the school suddenly decided it was "cool" to hit himself in the head with a two-by-four, how many kids would automatically do it too? What about drinking or drugs—do some kids get involved with these activities just to be cool?

- Have you ever had someone "make you sit at another table" because of your faith? If so, why do you think it happened? If not, why do think that's never happened to you?

- Jerry Lewis, the comedian and telethon host, once said, "You may as well learn to like yourself. Just think of how much time you're going to have to spend with you." What do you think this means? How can we learn to like ourselves? What does God have to do with learning to like yourself?

- How can we encourage each other to be our true selves? What are five things you could do this week to help people you know (or don't know) be true to who they really are?

CLOSING PRAYER:

Creator God, you made us all individuals. We are unique. The Bible says we are the highest form of your creation. Forgive us when we treat each other like we don't matter. Help us lift each other up and see the light that exists in every one of us. Amen.

OPTIONAL EXTRA

Prior to the meeting, make up blue ribbons or trophies for each of your students. Make sure each award is totally unique and suited to the person. Another possibility is to have each of your youth design an award for someone else. Let each person draw another group member's name from a hat and make an award for that person.

TOON TRIVIA

This is the first and only episode of *SpongeBob SquarePants* in which Patrick has a mailbox. It is also the first time we learn that Patrick's last name is Star.

66

SERIES
SpongeBob SquarePants

EPISODE
Boss Boots

VOLUME TITLE:
Tide & Seek

THEMES: Authority, Change, Friendship, Work

SCRIPTURES:

■ Psalm 98: God does not make mistakes. Everything (and everyone) is good.

■ Philippians 2:12-15: Tired? Ask God. It works better than caffeine.

■ Colossians 3:23: Ultimately, God is in charge—not you.

SYNOPSIS:

Pearl remodels "The Krusty Krab" into a hip trendy hangout. SpongeBob worries obsessively about the fate of his beloved restaurant—and his job.

DISCUSSION QUESTIONS:

▶ Who do you tend to like to work with more, men or women?

▶ Have you ever had to be the boss of a friend? Has a friend ever been your boss? Talk about that.

▶ What makes a good boss?

▶ What is the difference between micro-management and macro-management? Which kind of oversight do you prefer if you are the employee? Which kind do you prefer if you are the boss? Explain.

▶ Why is change hard? Who adapts to change better—teens or adults? Males or females?

▶ What is the hardest thing you ever had to quit doing? Why was it difficult? What happened when you tried to quit?

- Could you work at a job that required you to humiliate yourself? How much would it take for you to wear an animal suit?
- What is so great about changing to keep up with the times? What's wrong with tradition? Should some things just be left alone? Explain.
- Is your church contemporary or traditional? Do you wish it were more contemporary? More traditional?

CLOSING PRAYER:

God of change and tradition, so much is going on in the world around us. Things don't stay the same, and it gets confusing sometimes. Sometimes it feels like we are caught in a hurricane. You are the rock, God. When the winds blow, remind us to cling to you. When life is confusing, help us remember that you are always there. Amen.

 OPTIONAL EXTRA

Serve a precooked crab cake with this episode. (If you are feeling daring, insert a cloves into mini-marshmallows and give "eyes" to each crab cake.)

67

SERIES
SPONGEBOB SQUAREPANTS

EPISODE
MERMAID MAN AND BARNACLE BOY III

VOLUME TITLE:
TIDE & SEEK

THEMES: Goodness, Temptation

SCRIPTURES:

- Exodus 33:19: God is good. We should be good too.
- Psalm 119:73-80: God helps make us who we are.
- James 1:2-4: Whatever doesn't kill you makes you stronger.

SYNOPSIS:

SpongeBob and Patrick are placed in charge of Mermaid Man's cave and "accidentally" free one of Mermaid Man's most diabolical enemies—the evil ManRay.

DISCUSSION QUESTIONS:

- Why did SpongeBob free ManRay?
- Was the situation SpongeBob's fault? Who should take responsibility for it?
- What is the story of Pandora's Box? How is that story similar to this cartoon?
- Why does the "bad stuff" in life often appear to be more fun than what's good?
- How do you think the orb of confusion worked in the cartoon? Is there anything that works that way on you?
- What happens when we try to bury things inside ourselves?
- Read the parable of the prodigal son (Luke 15:11-31). Instead of thinking of the sons as representing two kinds of people, imagine that each son represents a different side of yourself. How does that change the story?

▶ Can bad people change? Are there some people who are just bad by nature? Did God create bad people?

CLOSING PRAYER:

God of all things, there is good and evil in this world. We may not completely understand why, but we know you are in charge of it all. Help us be whole. Amen.

TOON TRIVIA

The voice of ManRay in this episode is done by John Rhys-Davies, who starred as Indy's friend Sala in the *Indiana Jones* movies and as the dwarf, Gimli, in the *Lord of the Rings* trilogy.

 OPTIONAL EXTRA

Play a game of Tickle Belt. Make a "tickle belt" out of construction paper. Have the members of your group take turns wearing the belt and see if the rest of the group can make the person wearing the belt laugh—without touching him or her. Give a prize to the person who can keep a straight face the longest.

SERIES
SpongeBob SquarePants

EPISODE
Rock-a-bye Bivalve

VOLUME TITLE:
Tide & Seek

68

THEMES: Parents, Responsibility

SCRIPTURES:

■ Psalm 143: Parenting takes time to learn.

■ Luke 14:16-19: "I have responsibilities" often means you are avoiding responsibility.

■ Hebrews 12:15: Parenting—the job that never ends.

SYNOPSIS:

SpongeBob and Patrick find a baby and decide to become parents, completely unaware of the amount of responsibility they are taking on. SpongeBob feels like he's doing all the work himself.

DISCUSSION QUESTIONS:

▶ Why do you think SpongeBob and Patrick thought parenting would be easy? What did they learn?

▶ This toon gave us some pretty typical stereotypes of parental roles. Can you think of other TV shows that do the same?

▶ Often, movies and TV shows are willing to portray a mom as a corporate executive, but dads are still often seen as buffoons in the kitchen. Why do you think that is?

▶ What are a good mom's duties? What about a good dad?

▶ What makes a good parent?

▶ What is your role in the family? How has it changed?

- Who works hardest in your family?
- Is taking care of a baby more difficult than taking care of a teenager? Do you need "taking care of"?
- Read the Scripture from Luke. What are your responsibilities (not chores) that you have as part of a family?
- What kinds of things have you said to your parents to get out of work at home?
- What is the perfect age to become a parent? Explain.
- What is the hardest part about being a parent? What's the best part?
- When do you see yourself becoming a parent?
- What kind of parent will you be? What's the one thing you will never do to your kids?

TOON TRIVIA

At the end of the episode, the line, "Let's have another baby" was edited out for U.S. television audiences. Censors thought parents would think it was a sexual reference.

CLOSING PRAYER:

God, love us for who we are. Forgive us when we break the rules. Teach us what we need to know, and support us as we try to do it. Amen.

 OPTIONAL EXTRA

Borrow some dolls from the church nursery and have a speed-diapering contest. Or have kids bring in their baby pictures, post these on the wall, and see if the kids can guess who is who.

69

SERIES
SPONGEBOB SQUAREPANTS

EPISODE
SQUIRREL JOKES

VOLUME TITLE:
TIDE & SEEK

THEMES: Making Fun of Others, Self-esteem

SCRIPTURES:

- Romans 5:1-4: God is waiting to speak. We need to listen.
- 1 Corinthians 13:4-5: R-E-S-P-E-C-T.
- Titus 3:8: Sometimes you have to do what is right—even if it is not fun.

SYNOPSIS:

SpongeBob becomes a sensation as a comedian by telling squirrel jokes, totally unaware that he his hurting his good friend, Sandy.

DISCUSSION QUESTIONS:

▷ Have you ever had someone make fun of you?

▷ Years ago it was common for TV comedians to tell jokes making fun of particular ethnic groups. In the 1930s, there was a show called *Amos & Andy* that made fun of African Americans. Even today, there are shows and comedians who make a living putting down others. Why do some people like jokes aimed at putting down other people?

▷ Is there a point where we should just say "It's a joke. Don't take it so seriously"?

▷ Is an insulting comment okay if we say, "Hey, I was only joking"?

▷ What is bigotry?

▷ Why do we make fun of others? If we put a group of little kids in a small room, do you think they will eventually find one member of the group to pick on? Have you ever been the one who got picked on? Do you think we grow out of that?

▶ Can you be funny without putting someone down?

▶ Does everyone need someone to hate? Is that part of human nature?

▶ Could you give up fame and fortune if you knew it would come at the expense of a close friend? What if it were hurtful to your parents? What if it hurt a complete stranger?

▶ How does the Bible call us to treat each other?

▶ Do you think Jesus was a funny guy?

TOON TRIVIA

On television, this episode is often seen with "Mermaid Man and Barnacle Boy 3." In MM & BB3 we get to see SpongeBob's skeleton, yet in "Squirrel Jokes" he says he has no bones! Hmmmmmm...

CLOSING PRAYER:

All-loving and all-seeing God, help us laugh at ourselves. Help us build each other up, rather than taking each other down. Help the words not hurt so much. Amen.

OPTIONAL EXTRA

Let your group tell some youth minister jokes. (Be thick-skinned about this, and don't respond with teenager jokes. Just let them goof around a bit.) They can use any of the "dumb blonde" jokes and insert "youth minister." Start a round of "You know you're a youth minister if..."

SERIES
TEEN TITANS

EPISODE
DEEP SIX

VOLUME TITLE:
VOLUME 2: SWITCHED

THEMES: Ego, Teamwork

SCRIPTURES:

- Isaiah 33:15-16: Attitude is everything.
- Romans 12:1-3: Don't be perfect. Be yourself.
- James 1:2-5: Whatever doesn't kill you makes you stronger.

SYNOPSIS:

The Titans enlist the help of a water-breathing teen to help them stop the villain Trident. Along the way Aqualad and Beast Boy must put aside their egos in order to save the ocean.

DISCUSSION QUESTIONS:

▷ What was Beast Boy's problem?

▷ If cloning were legal, would you ever want to clone yourself? What famous person in history would you like to "bring back"?

▷ You've heard the expression "There's no 'I' in team." But are there some things that should be done alone?

▷ Do you know people who like to do everything themselves? What is it like to be around them?

▷ Would you rather work alone, or as part of a team? Would you rather work by yourself without getting any recognition, or as part of team that gets rewarded?

- Do we need recognition? Is it part of human nature? Do some people need recognition more than others?

- Has your ego ever gotten you into trouble? Isn't self confidence a good thing?

- When does self-confidence become egotism? When does it become dangerous? When does it get in the way of our relationship with God?

- Read Matthew 5:23-26. What do you think Jesus would say to Beast Boy and Aqualad?

- What kind of Teen Titan would Jesus be? (This question is just for fun—but toss it out there and see what happens!)

TOON TRIVIA

Special guest Titan Aqualad (looking quite a bit different from his previous cartoon self in the 1970s) is voiced by Wil Wheaton, who appeared as Wesley Crusher on *Star Trek: The Next Generation*.

CLOSING PRAYER:

God, help us put others before ourselves. Your son gave the ultimate sacrifice, but sometimes we complain if we have to let someone in front of us in line. Help us put aside our egos and support each other. Let us grow together and, in doing so, grow closer to you. Amen.

 OPTIONAL EXTRA

Have the members of your group make paper boats. (Pattern is available at *http://www.nagpurcity.net/netzine/980815a1.html*.) Then float them in a nearby body of water (or kiddie pool). From a distance, have the youth try to sink each other's boats with rocks or apples. Last boat floating is the winner.

71

SERIES
TEEN TITANS

EPISODE
FORCES OF NATURE

VOLUME TITLE:
VOLUME 1: DIVIDE AND CONQUER

THEMES: Bullies, Power, Siblings, Vandalism

SCRIPTURES:

- Proverbs 3:29-33: Twisted souls.
- Jeremiah 8:4-13: It's like banging your head against the wall.
- Ephesians 5:11: Don't keep it inside. Tell someone.

SYNOPSIS:

Two brothers (Thunder and Lightning) appear from another dimension and begin to wreak havoc on earth. The Titans must stop the pair and convince them that their "fun" isn't fun at all for others.

DISCUSSION QUESTIONS:

▷ Has your school ever been vandalized? Your car? Your house? Talk about it. How did you feel when you saw it?

▷ Why do some people think it's fun to break things? Is "breaking things" the attraction, or is it "breaking things that belong to someone else"? It is a matter of "if I can't have it, you can't either"?

▷ Is this kind of destructive behavior something that most people outgrow? Do you know someone who hasn't outgrown it? (No names, please.)

▷ Have you ever done something destructive?

▷ What sort of vandalism can be done to a person's soul? Is that damage harder to clean or fix?

- What gives you your sense of power? How much power do you have over your own life on a normal day?

- How can we learn to use the power we are given responsibly?

- What happens when a person is given a bit of power (for example, a driver's license) and that person abuses or messes it up (for example, a speeding ticket)? Why is it often difficult to regain that power?

- Most of us are given a massive amount of trust each day. We get up, we go to school, we do our homework. We are expected to do these things. We are trusted not to throw rocks at cars, steal things from stores, and punch strangers. Yet a small percentage of people break these rules and violate this trust. Why do you think that happens?

- Do children see vandalism differently from teenagers? Do teens see it differently from adults?

- Does vandalism imply a lack of self-respect? What can you do to help prevent it?

TOON TRIVIA

The scene where the giant orb goes rolling through the plaza certainly looks like a nod to the movie *Fight Club*.

CLOSING PRAYER:

God, we gain nothing by bringing others down. Even just a little brokenness—whether in a soul or a window—is damaging. Help us build each other up instead of knocking each other down. Help us find and feel your presence in us, and to show others that you exist in them too. Amen.

 OPTIONAL EXTRA

Starfire says to Beast Boy, "On my planet we have names for wrongdoers like you. You're a CLORBAG VARBLERNELK!!" Have your group decide what that means in English (but keep it clean!). Since there's no real Tamarind language, you'll have to be the judge on who is closest. Then ask your group to get creative and invent a translation for these other earth phrases in Tamarind: "Shut up." "Objects in the mirror may be closer than they appear." "What Would Jesus Do?"

72

SERIES
TEEN TITANS

EPISODE
NEVERMORE

VOLUME TITLE:
VOLUME 1: DIVIDE AND CONQUER

THEMES: Maturity, Self-image

SCRIPTURES:

- Psalm 3: God is an invisible force field.
- Mark 4:26-28: Seeds grow. What are you planting?
- Ephesians 4:12-16: Get it together and grow up.

SYNOPSIS:

The Titans worry about Raven after she loses her temper and shows Dr. Light something very scary. Beast Boy and Cyborg sneak into Raven's room and accidentally wind up in her mind. There they meet many different sides of Raven's personality. It is only when all the Ravens combine that they defeat the enemy, at least for now.

DISCUSSION QUESTIONS:

▸ Where is your place of refuge, your sanctuary?

▸ Raven seems to be the only Titan (so far) who has any sort of a spiritual life. Yet she is also the most gloomy. What do you think this means?

▸ Is Raven a goth? How would she fit in at your school? your church? your youth group?

▸ How many different Ravens were there?

▸ Make a list of seven different "yous"—one for each color. How do these different pieces of yourself come together?

- The title of this episode is "Nevermore," the oft-repeated word in Edgar Allen Poe's famous poem, "The Raven." Do you think this is an appropriate title? (Note: You can find the text of the poem at *http://raven.fanatique.net*)

- What is the monster? Do you have a monster? (If you feel comfortable, share it.)

- How does Raven defeat her monster?

- Have you ever known someone who can be a completely different person depending on the situation or whom they are with? Why does this happen?

- Read the parable of the Good Samaritan (Luke 10:30-37). What if this parable is like this episode of Teen Titans, and we are all of the characters? How does that change the meaning for you?

- What happens when we try to be different things for different people? How can we bring together the "Ravens" in our own lives?

- Think bigger. What if this story is about the many religions in our world? All religious faiths started in the same place, but have divided and often have little to do with each other. People of different faiths sometimes go to war because of their differences. Even Christians struggle to get along. How can we come together again?

CLOSING PRAYER:

God, we are all colors, but there are parts of each of us that we don't share or that we hide from the world. Help us pull ourselves together. Help us become one in ourselves, and one with you. Amen.

 OPTIONAL EXTRA

Download a picture of Raven from *http://titanstower.com/source/animated/00indexanimated.html* and print several copies out on cardboard door hangers. (They are easily purchased at any office supply store.) If possible, print the pictures out in black and white and let your students color them in according to which Raven they think they are.

SERIES
TEEN TITANS

EPISODE
SISTERS

VOLUME TITLE:
VOLUME 2: SWITCHED

THEMES: Family, Siblings

SCRIPTURES:

- Psalm 50: We all get what we deserve. Eventually.
- Proverbs 11:29: Don't mess with the family.
- 1 John 2:9-11: Learn to love, not hate, or the flashlight will go out. Then what?

SYNOPSIS:

Starfire's sister drops by for a visit, and we soon learn that the two have never gotten along very well. When Blackfire gets involved in the lives of the other Titans, Starfire begins to feel the same old hurt of being second to her sister. Eventually, Blackfire's real purpose is revealed, and Starfire shows what she's made of.

DISCUSSION QUESTIONS:

- If you have one or more sisters or brothers, do you get along with them? Do you know any siblings who get along like they are best friends? Do you know any who simply cannot stand each other? (No names, please.)

- Why do you think siblings often try to outdo each other? How does the anything-you-can-do-I-can-do-better philosophy apply?

- What causes jealousy between siblings?

- Who has a tougher time, older or younger siblings?

- Do sisters fight differently from brothers? Do they get along differently?

- As blended families become more prevalent, how do sibling relationships change?

- Read Colossians 3:12-14. God asks us to clothe ourselves in love. Does that sound easy or hard? How could it apply to the relationship between Starfire and Blackfire? How can it apply to your family relationships?

- Do you have aunts or uncles? What was their relationship like with your parents when they were teens? What is it like now?

- Why does it seem as if some people can't like themselves unless they are making someone else feel bad?

- Is this sibling rivalry, or just plain bullying?

- Even at the end of the program, Blackfire still blames her sister for her troubles. Have you ever known an everything-is-someone-else's-fault person?

- What's it like to deal with that person? Can you change that attitude? Why, or why not?

TOON TRIVIA

The comic book version of Blackfire was a bit more intense than the one depicted here. In the comic book, Blackfire killed Starfire's pet, betrayed the home planet to the nasty aliens, and sold her sister into slavery.

CLOSING PRAYER:

God, we are all sisters and brothers. We are all your children. Help us get past the petty things that separate us. Bring us together. Help us celebrate each other in the good times and work through the bad times together. Make us a family, God. Amen.

OPTIONAL EXTRA

Break your group into teams. Provide paper and pencil and see how many famous sisters each team can come up with in three minutes. At the end of the time, have the teams read their lists. Any entries appearing on both lists cancel each other out. The team with the most left wins. Play a second round with brothers.

SERIES
TEEN TITANS

EPISODE
SWITCHED

VOLUME TITLE:
VOLUME 2: SWITCHED

THEMES: Accepting Differences, Teamwork

SCRIPTURES:

- 1 Corinthians 12:12-27: If we're going to do this, we have to work together.
- Ephesians 5:21: It's all about give and take. Do both.
- Colossians 3:7-11: You know how to live right. Just do it.

SYNOPSIS:

When the boys' "souls" are transferred into wooden puppets, Starfire and Raven must rescue their teammates. But (surprise!) they find they've been switched to each other's bodies. The two must learn to understand each other before they can save their friends.

DISCUSSION QUESTIONS:

▸ Describe yourself as a toy. (I am like a _____, because I _____.)

▸ How do you picture your soul? Do you think it looks like some ghostly version of you? When does it leave?

▸ Do you believe in a "bodily resurrection" or does your soul go to eternity and leave the body behind?

▸ Do you think men work better with other men than with women? Would you rather have a man or a woman as your boss?

▸ Do men tend to work out their differences differently from women? Is one way better than another?

- Why is it hard to see things from someone else's point of view? Why do we tend to make judgments about each other instead of taking the time to understand each other?

- Have you ever talked about your religious beliefs with someone of another faith? What was that like?

- Is it possible for two Christians to approach their lives and beliefs in very different ways? Should everyone who follows Jesus agree about everything?

- Can you think of a time when you found out that you had totally misjudged someone?

- Imagine you are a puppet. Who is holding your strings? At what point should a puppeteer let go?

- Have you ever argued with someone and changed your thinking because of their argument? Talk about that.

- Have you ever watched a political debate on TV? What's the difference between a debate and an argument?

- What does it take for you to see someone else's side of an issue?

TOON TRIVIA

The character of the Puppet King looks and sounds a bit like an actor from the 1930s named Peter Lorre. Lorre's likeness was also used as the evil scientist in several Bugs Bunny cartoons.

CLOSING PRAYER:

God, you gave us ears as well as a mouth. Help us listen. You gave us eyes as well as a brain. Help us to see and to think. Help us learn not to shut others out because we disagree with them. Amen.

 OPTIONAL EXTRA

Write the names of those attending on separate pieces of paper. Have each kid draw a slip of paper, and on the word "go" have each one walk around the room pretending to be that person. (Emphasize the need for kindness, so that it doesn't embarrass anyone.) See if others can guess whose name is on the slip of paper. Be sure to put the name of the youth leaders in the batch just for fun.

75

SERIES
TEEN TITANS

EPISODE
TRANSFORMATION

VOLUME TITLE:
VOLUME 2: SWITCHED

THEMES: Being Yourself, Change, Growing Up, Physical Changes, Puberty, Rites of Passage

SCRIPTURES:

- Psalm 139: I am someone important. God said so.
- Jeremiah 18:6-11: God is the potter; we are the clay.
- Ephesians 4:12-16: Growing up is part of the whole "servant" thing.

SYNOPSIS:

Starfire is undergoing "transformation"—a process that all those of her race go through. No two transformations seem the same. Starfire grows horns. Unfortunately, there's a scary monster who thinks that Tamerians in transformation are quite the delicacy. Starfire's friends must let her know she is loved no matter what and help her defeat the big nasty.

DISCUSSION QUESTIONS:

▸ This episode is about puberty. These changes that all of us go through may seem monstrous to us, but it's all part of becoming who we are. Where do you get most of your information about puberty and the changes you are going through?

▸ How easy is it to talk about "sexual stuff" with your parents?

▸ Have you ever gotten a big honkin' zit in the middle of your forehead or on the end of your nose?

▸ Starfire says, "When my sister went through transformation, she turned purple for two days." Why does it seem like some people "blossom," while others go through their transformation like a car wreck?

- At puberty, voices change, feet grow, breasts appear, hair grows in strange places, emotions run a roller coaster—in short, each of us becomes something new. Why would God allow something this horrible to happen to us?

- How do parents change when their kids start going through puberty?

- In addition to great physical change, these years are also a time when we rely less, physically and emotionally, on our parents and more on ourselves. Many parents have trouble with that change. How can you talk with your parents and tell them they are still important to you while at the same time exploring this greater sense of freedom and responsibility?

- What happens to Starfire in the end? *(The "monstrous changes" subside and she is left with a new superpower.)* What superpowers do normal humans gain after puberty? What responsibilities go along with that?

TOON TRIVIA

The little bug that says "Help me" is a reference to the movie *The Fly* starring Vincent Price. Price once commented that the scene featuring the fly with the human head took hours to film because he giggled every time an offstage voice said "Help me."

CLOSING PRAYER:

God, we are not monsters. We are not hideous creatures. We are your creations, and we know you do not make mistakes. We are becoming. We are transforming into something new. Stay with us, God. Help us be transformed spiritually as well as physically. Help us become your servants. Amen.

 OPTIONAL EXTRA

Serve Pimple Poppers as a snack, using the recipe below. The ingredients you'll need are: Green and black olives (whole), Cheese Wiz, and green food coloring. (Alternate ingredients include cherry tomatoes and cream cheese.)

Carefully core the olives with a potato peeler. Using a small knife, stuff the holes with the Cheese Wiz. You can color some of the Cheese Wiz with the green food coloring. Demonstrate the proper way to eat Pimple Poppers by holding them up to your mouth and pinching them. It's also fun to draw a face on a clean piece of kitchen paper and smash the "pimples" on the drawn face before serving.

HELPFUL GUIDES

WHERE CAN I FIND THESE CARTOONS ON VIDEO?

PART 1: CLASSIC CARTOONS

Lesson 1	*The Flintstones: Season One*
Lesson 2	*The Jetsons: The Complete First Season*
Lessons 3-22	*Looney Tunes: The Golden Collection*
Lessons 23-24	*Peanuts: The Holiday Collection*
Lesson 25	*Scooby Doo, Where Are You? The Complete 1st and 2nd Seasons*
Lessons 26-27	*Tom & Jerry's Festival of Fun*
Lessons 28-29	*Walt Disney Treasures: Mickey Mouse in Color, Volume 2*

PART TWO: CURRENT CARTOONS

Lesson 30	*Aqua Teen Hunger Force, Volume One*
Lesson 31	*Aqua Teen Hunger Force, Volume Two*
Lessons 32-34	*Dexter's Laboratory: Greatest Adventures*
Lesson 35	*Futurama, Volume 3*
Lessons 36	*Justice League Unlimited: Joining Forces*
Lesson 37	*King of the Hill: Season 1*
Lessons 38-40	*King of the Hill: Season 3*
Lesson 41	*Pinky and the Brain: World Domination Tour*
Lessons 42-46	*Powerpuff Girls: Bubblevicious (VHS);*
	Powerpuff Girls: Powerpuff Bluff (DVD)
Lesson 47	*Roger Rabbit: The Best of Roger Rabbit*
Lessons 48-53	*Samurai Jack: The First Season*
Lessons 55-57	*The Simpsons: The Complete First Season*
Lesson 58	*The Simpsons: The Complete Third Season*
Lessons 59-61	*The Simpsons: The Complete First Season*
Lessons 54, 62	*The Simpsons: The Complete Second Season*
Lessons 63-64	*The Simpsons: The Complete First Season*
Lessons 65-69	*SpongeBob SquarePants: Tide & Seek*
Lessons 71-73	*Teen Titans: Volume 1, Divide and Conquer*
Lessons 70, 74-75	*Teen Titans: Volume 2, Switched*

INDEX OF SCRIPTURES REFERENCED

INDEX OF SCRIPTURES REFERENCED

Index of Scriptures Referenced

Index of Lesson Themes

INDEX OF LESSON THEMES

(CARTOONS LISTED BY LESSON NUMBER)